FISH FOR THOUGHT

An Eco-Cookbook

ARSENAL PULP PRESS

VANCOUVER

ARSENAL PULP PRESS
103-1014 Homer Street
Vancouver, B.C.
Canada V6B 2W9
www.arsenalpulp.com

The publisher gratefully acknowledges the support of the Government of Canada
through the Book Publishing Industry Development Program for its publishing activities.

Book design by Lisa Eng-Lodge
Production Assistant Felicia Lo
Food photography by Greg Athans
Food styling by Nathan Fong
Chapter page photos courtesy of Photodisc
Printed and bound in Canada

CANADIAN CATALOGUING IN PUBLICATION DATA:
Main entry under title:
Fish for thought

 ISBN 1-55152-081-8

1. Cookery (Seafood) 2. Sustainable fisheries. I. Living Oceans Society.
TX747.F57 2000   C41.6'92   C00-911002-X

THIS BOOK IS DEDICATED
TO ALL THE PEOPLE WHO
ARE WORKING TO ENSURE
A HEALTHY OCEAN AND
SUSTAINABLE FISHERIES FOR
FUTURE GENERATIONS.

C O N T E N T S

INTRODUCTION

Living Oceans Society is a non-profit organization working to conserve the marine life and habitat of our oceans. Based in the fishing village of Sointula on British Columbia's central coast, we are sensitive to coastal communities' economic dependency on the ocean. Consequently, we work to promote conservation initiatives that include people as part of the environment and advance economic and ecological sustainability.

The projects we work on are many. We currently work with fishermen to identify candidate marine-protected areas that can benefit their fisheries. We also work to raise awareness of the potential negative impacts of new industries such as open netcage salmon farming and offshore oil and gas. And through publications such as this cookbook, we promote sustainable fisheries. In addition, Living Oceans Society works with recreational divers to collect data about fish and invertebrates, thereby increasing our knowledge of the ocean.

The idea for *Fish for Thought* came about as a result of the 1998 commercial salmon fishing season. Although sockeye runs were low and some coho runs were in trouble, the chum salmon fishery was plentiful. However, since it is widely believed that sockeye is the only salmon worth eating, the demand for chum was almost non-existent. At the same time, many people were talking about not eating salmon at all because they had heard that the stocks were near extinction. Consequently, prices were lower, processing plants stopped buying, and fishermen were forced to quit their trade, even though there was plenty of chum salmon to catch. It became obvious that many people did not understand the complex and far-reaching issues of conservation that surround commercial fishing industries, particularly in British Columbia.

Fish for Thought is a cookbook designed to demystify the various conservation issues while at the same time provide exciting new ways to prepare your favourite seafood. It is our intention to help you understand that the seafood you buy affects local fishermen, coastal communities, and the overall health of our ocean. It is our hope that by reading about fishermen and trying their favourite recipes, you will feel a connection to them the next time you choose to purchase seafood at your local market or fishmonger.

This book comes at a time when many of the fisheries on the west coast are in trouble. While there are many factors that contribute to this decline, there are also conservation measures that help to develop sustainable fisheries. In order to convey the current health of each fishery, we have developed a rating system based on government-produced stock status reports. Each chapter starts with a rating of zero, one, two, or three fish, in which "zero" means an endangered species that should not be caught or eaten, and "three" is a species that is plentiful and therefore safe to catch or eat. The rationale for this rating is provided in the chapter along with some conservation tips, which reveal how you can play an active role in improving the management of our fisheries.

The fishermen included in this book have been chosen for their dedication to maintaining healthy fish stocks for our future. Like all of us, fishermen are a diverse group with many opinions and approaches toward sustainable fishing practices. (Note that in this book, we use the term "fishermen" to describe those who make their living from fishing, both male and female.) Although the ideas expressed and promoted here are not shared by everyone, the goal of long-term stocks for our future is the same. Fishing is not only a means to make a living; it is a unique way of life passed down through generations. This book provides you with recipes from these fishermen—the people who know the product best—as well as brief glances into their lives. Also included are recipes from others who share in the concern for the health of our ocean—from food critics to award-winning chefs to internationally known entertainers. We have also included a wide spectrum of recipes from quick and easy to elegant.

In British Columbia, fish are part of a much larger ecosystem that extends from Alaska to northern California. Migratory fisheries are jointly managed by Canada and the United States. The albacore troll fleet and the Pacific halibut long line fleet have commissions with representation from both Canada and the U.S., and the salmon fishery is managed through a treaty between both countries. Although other species in the book are considered relatively sedentary and are managed separately by each country, the same species frequent American waters and in most cases the issues are relevant to both countries. However, with a little knowledge and some delicious recipes, we discuss fisheries from a Canadian perspective, and much like the fish themselves, many of the issues cross both political and geographical boundaries.

Whether you live near the sea, on the prairies, or high in the mountains, your shopping dollar can help the fish and fishermen of our beloved oceans. The choices that you make as a consumer are powerful ones. We hope this book provides you with the information you need to make the right decisions.

Clams

CLAMS

Nothing soothes the soul like a hearty bowl of clam chowder on a rainy day, or frying up a plate of fritters using clams you have just dug up on your local beach. But clams provide more then just a satisfying seafood meal; they also help to naturally clean our ocean waters. Clams feed by filtering tiny plants and animal particles from the water. In areas where there are high levels of pollution, clams will also filter out toxins.

In British Columbia, pollution from municipal sewage and storm water outfalls, faulty septic fields, and discharges from vessels have resulted in 105,000 hectares currently closed to clam harvesting, an increase of thirty-one percent since 1993. These closures are warning signs that the quality of our oceans is diminishing. We shouldn't ignore these signs; good water is essential to the health of our coastal clam beds.

Clams have always played an important role in the lives of people on the west coast. The Coastal First Nations have used clams in a variety of ways. Shells were ground and used as powder for paint, and some villages dried clams on strips of cedar and used them

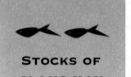

STOCKS OF CLAMS MAY BE ABUNDANT AT PRESENT, BUT POLLUTION HAS MADE SOME AREAS UNHARVESTABLE.

as currency. To this day, protecting clam beaches remains an important issue to First Nations.

The commercial clam industry began in the early 1800s. In 1882, whole Butter clams were processed in the Rivers Inlet Salmon Cannery and by the early 1900s, small coastal canneries were canning clams during the off-season. At present, there are 1,160 licensees for the commercial harvest of clams, with fifty percent belonging to First Nations.

Clams are among the longest living animals in the world. The Guinness Book of World Records reports that a thick-shelled specimen of the Atlantic clam collected in 1982 was found with 220 growth rings, indicating its age to be about 220 years old.

There are many different species of clams, but only a few are currently targeted commercially: these include the Manila, the Little Neck, and the Butter clam. Each species has different qualities which make it suitable for different cooking methods. Siphon lengths offer a valuable clue to the ocean depth where each particular species of clam can be found. For example, the Little Neck clam occurs near the surface and has a short siphon, whereas the Butter clam has a longer siphon and is found in deeper waters.

The most sought-after of clams is the Manila; they originated in Japan and were introduced to the west coast along with Pacific oysters in 1936. Since that time they have spawned and established wild populations from central B.C. to California, where they live in high intertidal zones. Burrowing just below the surface to a maximum depth of ten centimetres, the adult remains in the same location for life. They sexually mature at approximately two years of age, and on the west coast reach the legal harvestable size limit at about three to five years in the Strait of Georgia and five to six years on the North Coast. The Manila clam has become the most marketable clam due largely to its ability to remain fresh long after harvesting.

Butter clams are often used for chowders. They are found in waters off Southern Alaska to Central California, usually in the mid-intertidal zone. They sexually mature at about three years of age, and in B.C. reach legal harvestable size of 2.5 inches at approximately seven to eight years of age in the Strait of Georgia and nine years on the North Coast. Butter clams can live to be as old as twenty. They are harvested with pitch forks, as they can bury themselves as deep as eleven feet.

Pacific Little Neck clams are fast-growing, but are not as abundant as other clam species. They have been located in waters off Alaska to Southern California,

PARALYTIC SHELLFISH POISONING (PSP)

Shellfish harvesters should be aware of red tide. Red tide occurs when a certain species of phytoplankton reproduces to such a density that it colours the water reddish brown. However, like many toxic substances, red tide doesn't have to be visible to be toxic. Filter feeders such as clams and oysters tend to absorb a toxin produced by the phytoplankton. When a person eats the affected clams or oysters, the cumulative effect of the toxin attacks the central nervous system, resulting in great pain and discomfort, and in extreme cases, death.

Red tide is most likely to occur during the summer months. However, the safest way of knowing the health of a clam bed is by calling your local fisheries authority for information regarding red tide in your area.

1 When purchasing clams at the market or ordering them in a restaurant, ask if they know what company harvested them. Tell the vendor or server that you want clams that are legal size and from areas with clean water.

2 If you are concerned about the health of your local beaches, especially if you live in the Strait of Georgia or near an industrial waste outfall, express your concerns to your local government official.

and sexually mature at about the age of two. In B.C., the legal harvestable size of 1.5 inches is reached in three to five years in the Strait of Georgia and five to six years on the North Coast. Typically, these clams are used for steaming and in chowders. They do not always open when steamed and should be used quickly after harvesting.

Two major threats to the wild clam stocks are poaching and pollution. Legal size limits are set so that a clam has reproduced at least once before harvesting. However, poaching has included the harvesting of undersized wild clams as well as clams in closed areas. Harvesting clams before they have reached legal size can diminish the overall health of the clam bed, and those harvested in closed areas can pose obvious public health concerns due to pollution.

Clam farming is prevalent throughout the west coast. While clam farming is relatively clean, farmers are permitted to market all sizes of their product, whereas wild clams have legal limits. One of the challenges of managing the wild clam fishery is determining the origin of undersized clams. It is virtually impossible to detect where undersized clams have come from, unless poachers are caught in the act. The Canadian Department of Fisheries and Oceans has attempted to educate people frequenting clam beaches to keep an eye out for poachers and to contact officials if they have any suspicions. By purchasing your clams from a reputable source, you can ensure that they have been harvested according to conservation laws.

The intertidal clam harvest is small in comparison to most other fisheries. Still, it remains important to coastal communities culturally and economically, and continues to provide food and needed employment to these areas. Healthy clam beaches are a sign of good water quality, essential to the health of coastal communities.

*J*oanne Kates is best known as the restaurant critic for *The Globe and Mail*. Her concise and creative reviews of restaurants have played an influential role in the growth of the Toronto restaurant scene. Maintaining her anonymity to avoid preferential treatment, Joanne is heard but not seen every Saturday in *The Globe and Mail's* national edition. During the summer months, Joanne Kates is the director of Camp Arowhon in Algonquin Park, Ontario, where campers dine on exquisite meals delivered with prompt yet relaxed service. Here is Joanne's recipe for a delectable clam chowder. She says, "You may use fresh-shucked oysters for this recipe instead of clams, and then this becomes oyster stew. Whichever you choose, don't use canned seafood. If you can't get fresh clams or oysters, it's not worth making. Made properly, this is a main course soup. Served with salad and muffins, it's a fine meal."

Joanne Kates' Clam Chowder

2 large onions, chopped
3 tbsp. butter or 3 slices bacon, diced
2 medium potatoes, cubed
2 cups vegetable stock or water
1 bay leaf
¹/₄ tsp. thyme
¹/₂ tsp. salt

1 stalk celery (with leaves), chopped
2 cups meat from freshly shucked clams, coarsely diced
4 cups 18% cream
¹/₄ tsp. white pepper
Dash of paprika

In a saucepan, sauté onions in butter or with bacon, on medium low heat for about 20 minutes until sweet and golden but not brown. Add cubed potatoes to the onions and sauté for 10 minutes, stirring often so the potatoes don't stick. Add stock or water, bay leaf, thyme, and salt. Stir, then add chopped celery. Let simmer for 10 minutes uncovered until all the water has boiled away. Add the clams with their juice, cream, and pepper and bring back to a boil. Remove from heat. Sprinkle generously with paprika and serve.

Makes 6 servings.

$\mathcal{L}$eslie Lanqvist was born in Alert Bay on Vancouver Island, B.C. in 1932, not far from the town of Sointula, where he grew up. By the time Leslie was fifteen, he was running his own boat, fishing for salmon, halibut, clams, and many other species. Leslie, his wife Rita, and their three children Victor, Gregory, and Tammy have all enjoyed the fishing life. Together, Leslie and his brother Davie skippered the seine boat the

Photo by Rick James

Millionaires where they broke in many green deckhands.

Leslie was well-known for his hospitality. There was always room at the dinner table and there was usually something he had caught or hunted himself on the menu. He was a fine connoisseur of seafood and gladly shared his bounty with his friends and neighbours. Although Leslie is not with us today, he is remembered up and down the coast as a unique individual; those of us who dined with him have a special memory of his succulent clam fritters.

Leslie Lanqvist's Clam Fritters

2 cups ground clams (Butter clams are good but any kind will do)
$^1/_2$ cup flour
$^1/_2$ cup canned milk
1 tsp. Worcestershire sauce or soy sauce
Salt to taste
Pepper to taste
3 tbsp. vegetable oil

In a bowl, mix together clams, flour, milk, Worcestershire sauce, salt, and pepper. In a saucepan, heat the oil. Place spoonfuls of clam mixture into hot oil. Cook until fritters bounce off the bottom of the pan, then turn over to brown other side. When brown, place on rack to drain.

Makes 4 to 6 servings.

Photo by Kelly Edwards

*T*atiana Housty is the daughter of the hereditary Heiltsuk Chief Gary Housty of Bella Bella, B.C. After leaving Bella Bella, Tatiana studied in Australia, Asia, and France, earning a degree in media and communications. Tatiana is currently the host and producer of *First Story*, a Vancouver Television program on Canada's Aboriginal issues. Growing up in Bella Bella, clams were a big part of Tatiana's diet and she has brought her love for clams to her new life. The following is a recipe from her grandmother in Bella Bella.

Photo by Stacey Kuhn

Photo by Kelly Edwards

Tatiana Housty's Garlic and Scallion Clams

12 cloves fresh garlic
2 tbsp. green onions, minced
$\frac{1}{2}$ cup butter
$\frac{1}{4}$ cup vegetable oil
$\frac{1}{2}$ cup chopped parsley
1 tsp. dry Italian seasoning
1 cup dry white wine
1 cup clam juice
1 cup water
20 medium clams in the shell, scrubbed and rinsed

In a large skillet, sauté garlic, green onions, butter, and oil for 1 minute. Add parsley and seasoning and stir, then add wine, clam juice, and water. Cook for 2 minutes, then add clams and cook until clams open, about 10 to 12 minutes. Discard any clams that have not opened during cooking. Serve in bowls.

Makes 2 to 4 servings.

*D*on Genova is a radio personality, hosting shows such as *Pacific Palate* and *Food for Thought* on CBC Radio. Although listeners cannot see, taste, or smell what Don is cooking, he can still make your mouth water as he describes various food products from B.C. and abroad. Don also writes a column called "Pacific Palate" for MyBC.com and occasionally contributes to the *National Post*, *Homes West*, and *BC Business Magazine*. Following are two great recipes for steamed clams.

Photo by Kelly Edwards

Don Genova's Steamed Clams, Greek-Style

2 tbsp. olive oil
2 medium onions, chopped
4 cloves garlic, chopped
1 cup green or red peppers, chopped
1-28-oz. can tomatoes, including juice
Juice of half a lemon
$\frac{1}{2}$ cup red wine
1 tsp. each dried basil, thyme, and oregano
3 lbs. clams in the shell, scrubbed and rinsed
1 cup feta cheese, crumbled

In a large pot over medium heat, sauté onions in the oil. Add garlic and peppers and continue to sauté until they begin to get tender. Then add tomatoes (you can chop them a bit in the can with a long knife before you add them), lemon juice, wine, and dried herbs. Bring to a boil, then simmer for a few minutes before adding the clams. Cover pot and simmer until clams have opened. Discard any clams that have not opened during cooking. Stir in feta cheese just before serving. Serve in bowls with lots of fresh, crusty bread or buns.

Makes 6 servings.

Don Genova's Pacific Palate Steamed Clams, Chinese-Style

2 tbsp. vegetable oil
4 cloves garlic, chopped
5 $\frac{1}{4}$-inch slices fresh ginger, julienned
3 stalks green onions, chopped
2 tbsp. fermented black beans, rinsed and chopped
1 tsp. sesame oil
$\frac{1}{2}$ cup white wine
3 lbs. clams, scrubbed and rinsed

In a large, heavy-bottomed pot, heat vegetable oil. Sauté garlic, ginger, green onions, and black beans until mixture is fragrant, then add sesame oil and white wine, then clams. Cover pot and steam for 3 to 5 minutes, or until clams open. Discard any clams that haven't opened during cooking.

Makes 6 servings.

Farmed Salmon

FARMED SALMON

Everybody loves to eat salmon. Whether barbecued, smoked, steamed, or out of the can, salmon is a wonderful meal. However, shopping for salmon is not as straightforward as it used to be.

The emergence of the salmon farming industry over the past twenty years has produced fresh salmon all year round, making it an enticing choice for shoppers. It was originally thought that farming salmon would take pressure off our depleted wild salmon, but research has revealed that the opposite is true. Whereas wild salmon are born in rivers, live in the wild ocean, and are caught by fishermen, farmed salmon are raised in captivity with up to 20,000 fish per pen, fed processed food, and are susceptible to disease. Experience has shown us that farmed salmon are a threat to wild salmon, the coastal economy, our environment, and to public health.

In British Columbia, there are three species of farmed salmon: Chinook, Coho, and Atlantic. Eighty-one percent of the salmon farmed in B.C. are of the Atlantic variety, which is the cause of the greatest concern. Salmon farms are located close to the shore along the B.C. coast, the majority of which are in the Broughton Archipelago region. A typical farm covers about one

NO FISH: AFTER YOU READ WHAT WE HAVE TO SAY ABOUT FARMED FISH, YOU WON'T WANT TO EAT IT!

hectare of the ocean. Each farm uses from ten to thirty net cages, each cage being approximately forty-nine feet by ninety-eight feet. Up to 20,000 juvenile salmon are placed in each pen where they live out their life cycle, which varies due to market demands. About sixty-five percent of B.C.'s fish farms use predator net guards that hang down fifty feet into the ocean. Some farmers dip these nets in a highly toxic copper-based anti-foulant to prevent marine organisms from growing on them.

Coastal communities have developed a unique culture and heritage that value ecological and economic sustainability. Central to this philosophy is having traditional and emerging industries that ensure all revenue stays within the community. The fish farm industry, however, does not support this philosophy. Currently, there are seventy-nine fish farms along the B.C. coast owned by sixteen multinational companies that provide some low-paying jobs to the people in coastal communities. Most of the income generated flows to large city shareholders who have not expressed any long-term commitment to these communities. Furthermore, fish farms have a negative impact on traditional coastal industries, such as

Broughton Archipelago

commercial fishing. And they affect emerging industries such as tourism by restricting access to stretches of shoreline and sheltered anchorages that are so important to B.C.'s recreational boaters.

At present there is a ban on the expansion of the fish farm industry. However, the existing farms are still endangering our wild salmon. In 1998, it was reported that 80,975 adult and juvenile Atlantic salmon from farms escaped into B.C. waters. These Atlantic salmon are obviously not native to British Columbia waters and therefore compete with wild stocks for food and habitat. In September 1998, a B.C. government report

CONSERVATION TIPS

1 Next time you are at the market, don't let the words "Fresh Salmon" fool you. Make sure the vendor can assure you that the salmon is wild, not farmed. If they cannot guarantee this, order something different and tell them you will purchase salmon only if it is wild.

2 When dining in a restaurant, ask your server what kind of salmon is being served. Again, make sure it is wild salmon before you order. You won't regret it.

revealed that juvenile Atlantic salmon were found in the Tsitika River, an ecological reserve that is home to many resident Orca whales. Atlantic salmon reproduce much faster than wild salmon, and have the potential to increase their numbers dramatically. The presence of Atlantic salmon in rivers like the Tsitika means less food and spawning grounds for wild salmon, which will have a serious impact on the wild salmon's ability to reproduce and survive. Additionally, adult Atlantic salmon feed in fresh waters, and wild salmon eggs have been found in their stomachs.

In captivity, the high density of fish in the net pens often leads to outbreaks of disease. When farmed salmon become sick, antibiotics (the kind used to fight human infections) are given in the form of pellets. A large percentage of these pellets sink down to the ocean floor to be consumed by crabs, shrimp, prawns, bottom fish, and many other forms of sealife.

We only have to look around the world to see the impact of diseases being spread from farmed fish. In Norway, a parasite from salmon farms infested twenty-four Norwegian rivers. The government was forced to treat these rivers with a poison that wiped out all forms of life, including wild salmon. Today, for every four salmon caught in Norwegian waters, only one is wild. In Ireland, the collapse of wild sea trout is believed to be caused by the transfer of sea lice from farmed salmon to wild trout. Meanwhile, in Canada, a disease known as Infectious Salmon Anemia has wreaked

havoc on the New Brunswick fish farm industry. The provincial government ordered the slaughter of half a million farmed fish, paying out $10 million in compensation to the industry.

Public health is an important issue to consider when buying salmon. There are concerns that the heavy dosages of antibiotics used in fish farms may contribute to the new growth of drug-resistant bacteria. Public concerns about the use of antibiotics and chemicals in the food we eat are shown by the dramatic increase in organic food sales. In fact, the total organic food sales for Canada in 1997 is estimated at $500 to $600 million and is growing by twenty to twenty-five percent annually. By purchasing wild salmon, you are ensured that you are eating a wholesome, healthy organic food.

There are five different species of wild salmon: Chum, Coho, Pink, Sockeye, and Spring. Wild salmon thrive in the abundant pastures of the ocean. It is the constant movement of the wild salmon on their journey through this vast ocean that prevents outbreaks of disease. They spin a web of life from sea to stream during their life cycle: even their dead carcasses make a large contribution to our food chain, their decomposed bones providing nitrogen and other trace elements that fuel our forests and support the life chains of our streams. Wild salmon are vital to the cultures, small businesses, and families of coastal communities.

Salmon is a good source of protein and low in fat.

One of the main nutritional benefits of fish comes from the Omega-3 fatty acids it contains. Several reports, including those by the Canadian Department of Fisheries and Oceans and the *American Journal of Clinical Nutrition*, state that the levels of Omega-3 is higher in wild salmon than farmed salmon. Omega-3 fatty acids have been associated with lowered risk of heart disease and reduced incidence of breast cancer, and it may help ease the symptoms of manic depression. Therefore, eating wild salmon is a wise health decision.

In addition to its health benefits, wild salmon that is caught and processed naturally is also better tasting than the farmed salmon that is available "fresh" all year round. The chapter on wild salmon in this book provides information about how to support a sustainable wild salmon fishery and how to look for top quality fillets and steaks when you are shopping. Shakespeare might have been referring to salmon when he said, "In season, all is good." When shopping for fish, ask for wild salmon.

$\mathcal{A}$lexandra Morton—whale researcher, artist, author, environmentalist, and mother—lives in the Broughton Archipelago in the small community of Echo Bay, B.C. Alex moved to this area to study how whales communicate. When the first salmon farm appeared in her community, Alex was excited about the potential jobs for her neighbours. However, within a few short years, toxic blooms began staining the waters, and the local Coho hatchery became infected with a disease that originated at a nearby fish farm. When the whales started disappearing as a result of underwater noisemakers used on fish farms to control predators, Alex became a very active and constant voice in the fight to stop fish farms. The progress made today is a direct result of her commitment. Here is Alex's wonderful recipe for baked wild salmon.

Photo by Chris Bennet

Photo by Kelly Edwards

Alex Morton's Baked Wild Salmon

4 medium wild salmon fillets (5 oz. each)
1 cup yoghurt
1 cup mayonnaise
4 tbsp. soy sauce
2–4 garlic cloves, crushed
2 tbsp. hoisin sauce
2 tsp. mustard
Pepper to taste

Preheat oven to 350° F. In shallow baking dish, place salmon fillets and set aside. Mix together mayonnaise and yoghurt, then add remaining ingredients. Cover fillets with sauce and place in oven for approximately 10 minutes.

The salmon should flake when a fork is inserted into the thickest part. If not, return to oven until ready, checking every few minutes. As soon as it flakes, place fish under broiler to brown for a minute or two, taking care not to burn. Then enjoy one of the best tastes on the planet.

Makes 4 servings.

$\mathcal{B}$ radley Clease, born in Nanaimo, B.C., has been cooking professionally for eleven years. He says he learned a lot about food travelling through Europe and Southeast Asia. Bradley is committed to regional foods, and the use of organic products whenever possible. He has been Executive Chef at the Raintree at the Landing in Vancouver, B.C. for four years. He decided to move toward using wild salmon after educating himself on the environmental issues surrounding farmed fish. Since making the change, Bradley has found wild salmon to be superior to farmed fish. He remains committed and proud to be serving wild salmon.

Photo by Kelly Edwards

Bradley Clease's Grilled Wild Sockeye Salmon

1 cup organic carrot juice
1 tbsp. cornstarch
1 tbsp. balsamic vinegar
$\frac{1}{8}$ cup soapberry juice
$\frac{1}{8}$ cup +2 tbsp. cold water
1 oz. white sugar (to taste)
Salt to taste
4 wild salmon fillets (5 oz. each)
1 tbsp. mixed herbs (parsley, thyme, and basil)

Carrot sauce:
Heat the juice on low heat, ensuring it does not boil. Add 2 tablespoons of cold water to cornstarch and whisk together. Add cold-water mixture to heated carrot juice, whisk, salt slightly, and add balsamic vinegar.

Soapberry mousse:
In a cold, clean mixing bowl whisk soapberry juice, sugar, and the remaining $\frac{1}{8}$ cup of cold water until soft peaks are produced.

Set both sauces aside.

Over a barbecue, in a hot pan, or under a broiler, cook each wild salmon fillet for about three minutes or until preferred doneness.

Place salmon in middle of dinner plate. Spoon a little of each sauce on either side of fillet, keeping them separate for contrast. Sprinkle with chopped mixed herbs.

Makes 4 servings.

*P*eter Gzowski—author broadcaster, author, columnist, and champion of literacy—is well known for his fifteen years as host of CBC Radio's *Morningside*. In 1997, he moved on to many exciting things, including writer in residence for the CBC TV series *North of Sixty*, which meant spending much time in Canada's Arctic. Peter is now working on a book about the North, its people, and unique politics. Peter's column "Gzowski's Canada" can be read each month in *Canadian Living* magazine. Among his many outstanding accomplishments are seven Actra Awards, eleven honorary degrees, a membership in the Canadian Hall of Fame, and a companion of the Order of Canada. Peter takes great pride in a series of golf tournaments he founded in aid of literacy. To date, he has raised $6 million to benefit community-based literacy organizations. Here is one of Peter's favorite wild salmon recipes:

Photo by Kelly Edwards

Peter Gzowski's Lazy Salmon on a BBQ

1 whole wild salmon, cleaned
2 lemons sliced
6 garlic cloves, peeled
1 cup fresh dill
2 large tomatoes, quartered

Take one beautiful, cleaned wild salmon.

Open and stuff with lemon slices, whole garlic cloves, lots of fresh dill, and quartered ripe tomatoes.

Wrap in double foil place on barbecue.

Cook about 45 minutes turning once or so.

Unwrap throw stuffing away, eat salmon.

YUM!

*C*armen Burrows has been involved in many aspects of the fishing industry, including salmon seining and herring packing. Although she has dedicated the majority of her time during the past few years to her children Leo and Carlee, she has always taken time out of her busy schedule to voice her concerns about the harmful effects of fish farms on our coast. In June 2000, Carmen brought her children along when she and her father Bruce joined local First Nations in a flotilla of boats travelling the Broughton Archipelago to protest fish farming in that area. The following is a treasured recipe from Carmen's Grandma Win:

Grandma Win's Light and Fluffy Salmon Loaf

1 large onion, finely chopped
4 cups canned salmon
$^1/_2$ cup milk
3 tbsp. chopped parsley
2 tbsp. lemon juice
Dash worchesire sauce
Dash of salt
Dash of pepper
4 eggs, separated (whites)

Preheat oven to 350° F. Sauté onion and add to flaked salmon in a large bowl (do not drain juice). Add rest of ingredients except egg whites and mix. Beat egg whites until stiff and fold in. Put mixture in a buttered glass or Pyrex 9x11 baking dish. Bake for 45 minutes to 1 hour.

Makes 4–6 servings.

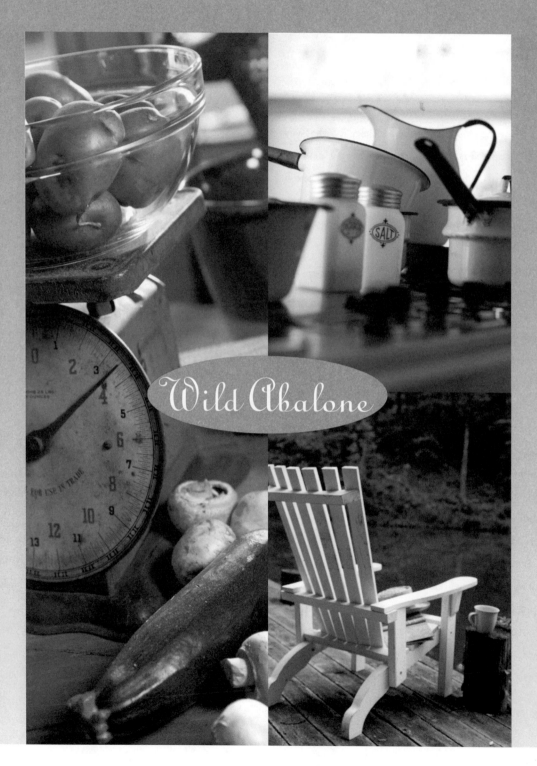

Wild Abalone

WILD ABALONE

The commercial abalone fishery on the west coast was very short-lived; in only nineteen years, the species became commercially extinct. This does not mean that abalone have totally disappeared from the west coast. In fact, you may see clusters of them if you go diving. However, abalone require special conditions in order to reproduce and, due to mismanagement of the fishery, these conditions have been seriously disrupted. Consequently, the fishery collapsed in 1991, and it is illegal to buy, sell, or harvest abalone in British Columbia. An understanding of the history, biology, and conservation issues surrounding abalone is essential to understanding why abalone stocks have reached such low levels.

Abalone are herbivores; they graze on seaweed and algae that cover rock surfaces. They live in subtidal environments attached to hard and rocky surfaces. Both male and female abalone spawn by congregating in large groups and expelling reproductive cells into the water. A critical mass of individuals are required to set off the spawning process. The larvae are dispersed in the water column and settle on the seabed, attaching themselves to a rock or a similar hard surface. Abalone then spend the rest of their lives on the same reef, moving from rock to rock in search of food. As they get older, they begin to feed on drifting algae in the ocean. Their shells and bodies grow about half an inch per year. The largest abalone on record was seven inches long. Natural predators include sea otters, fish, sea stars, crabs, and octopus, but some abalone are believed to live up to fifteen years of age.

In 1977, fisheries managers stopped selling abalone licenses, hoping to control the amount of abalone being caught. To try to build an understanding of these creatures, harvesters were required to keep track of all information in log books issued by the Canadian Department of Fisheries and Oceans. Despite these efforts, the stocks continued to fall, resulting in the closure of the B.C. abalone fishery. It is thought by many scientists that their collapse was due to over-fishing, which reduced the stocks to a point where they could no longer reproduce at a level that supported the fishery.

Excessive poaching prevents stocks from rebuilding and creating optimum reproduction conditions. Poaching has become a lucrative business as prices for illegal

> **NO FISH: HARVESTING WILD ABALONE IS CURRENTLY ILLEGAL. STOCKS ARE IN GRAVE DANGER IN B.C. AND DECLINING IN OTHER PARTS OF THE WORLD.**

abalone have reached as high as $50 a pound. Some believe that the amount of illegally caught abalone in 1999 is equal to the yearly catch of the legal fisheries in the past. Poaching is hard to control for several reasons. Most abalone beds are located in very isolated areas that are hard to monitor. The origin of the abalone is hard to prove, especially after it has left the country.

Since the collapse of the abalone fishery, many groups in British Columbia have tried to find solutions to rebuild stocks. Interested parties are working together in developing successful strategies toward a sustainable abalone fishery. Some of these include increasing enforcement, heavier penalties for illegal harvesting, transplanting stock into existing abalone beds, developing no-take marine protected areas (MPAs), and setting up abalone farms along the coast. A new weapon against poachers is a German shepherd named Dart, which has been trained to sniff out abalone aboard fishing vessels.

It is thought by most that the wild abalone is a fishery of the past; however, setting up MPAs that are strictly monitored will help to rebuild the stocks. Eventually, the abalone populations inside protected areas will be large enough to produce spawn that will help reseed areas outside of the MPA. In addition to replenishing stocks, no-take MPAs would give us a chance to study abalone in greater detail to gain insight into their reproductive cycles, eating habits, and behaviour.

In 1998, the Canadian and provincial governments made a commitment to establish a network of marine protected areas, but have not yet committed to any no-take areas. Living Oceans Society believes that the development of no-take areas is the key to creating

1 **DO NOT PURCHASE ABALONE.** Since abalone cannot be harvested in B.C. and many other parts of the world, chances are the abalone you purchased has been caught illegally. By refusing to purchase abalone you could help control poaching and contribute to the rebuilding the stocks.

2 Since we cannot eat abalone, we are keeping our abalone recipes secret. We hope the next time we write a cookbook the stocks will be stronger, allowing us to eat this delicious treat once again. Until then, we ask you to remember that all our fisheries can go the way of the abalone if we are not careful.

3 Write a letter to the Canadian Minister of Fisheries and Oceans or the government agency in your area urging the establishment of a network of marine protected areas with a core of no-take zones. (See sample letter in the Appendix.)

sustainable fisheries and we will continue to work with all governments, First Nations, and stakeholders to make this a reality.

Surveys have been conducted to determine whether the fishery should reopen, but to date there have been no indications of the stocks rebuilding. In other parts of the world, the abalone fishery continues while stocks decline. It is hoped that in B.C. we will gain the necessary knowledge to build up our abalone stocks

There are initiatives underway to farm abalone in an environmentally friendly manner. Although farmed abalone has yet to hit the market, it looks like a promising product. Stay tuned.

and once again be able to enjoy wild abalone for dinner. Until then, we recommend you protect abalone stocks and avoid buying or eating them altogether.

LIVING OCEANS

SOCIETY

Halibut

HALIBUT

The largest member of the flatfish family is the Pacific halibut, also know as the hippo of the sea (*Hippoglossus*). These monstrous fish, which can weigh hundreds of pounds, have a meaty, white flesh that is ideal for everything from stews to steaks to fish and chips. Some brave souls even eat the heads of the halibut (recipe provided-we dare you to try it out!).

Pacific halibut can be found in abundance in the coastal waters of the North Pacific Ocean, from Central California to the Northern Bering Sea. The greatest concentration of halibut occurs in the northern regions of British Columbia and southern areas of Alaska. The largest halibut recorded weighed in at 890 pounds and was caught off B.C.'s Queen Charlotte Islands.

Halibut larvae begin life with an eye on each side of the head. When they are about one inch long, the left eye moves around to the right side of the head and pigmentation on the left side fades. At about the age of six months, the halibut takes on the characteristic flatfish form and settles to the bottom of the ocean in shallow, in-shore areas. From this time on, both eyes

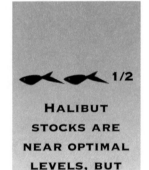

HALIBUT STOCKS ARE NEAR OPTIMAL LEVELS, BUT DECLINING SLIGHTLY.

reside on the top side of the fish, where they blend in with its mottled, grey-coloured skin (the underside is snow white). From above, the halibut looks like the ocean floor; from below, its whiteness can easily blend in with the sparkling light of the sun on the sea's surface. This camouflage provides excellent protection from predators.

Halibut reach maturity at ten to twelve years of age and spawn between the months of October to March. Most adult fish make a seasonal migration from the more shallow feeding grounds in summer to deeper spawning grounds in winter. A female halibut may release as many as 2.7 million eggs in her lifetime, although many become food for predators before reaching maturity. As larvae, they feed on plankton and move great distances with the ocean current. Juvenile halibut feed on small, shrimp-like animals and fish; as they grow, they subsist on a wide-ranging seafood diet that includes cod, sablefish, pollock, rockfish, sculpins, octopus, crabs, and clams.

Female halibut tend to be larger and live longer than their male counterparts. On average, females live up to thirty-five years and weigh 470 pounds. Males, on the other hand, live up to twenty-five years and weigh only about forty pounds. It is safe to say that any halibut over 100 pounds is likely to be a female halibut.

The halibut fishery is one of the oldest and best managed fisheries in B.C., dating back 100 years. The International Pacific Halibut Commission (IPHC), a joint Canada/U.S. initiative, was established in 1923, making this one of the longest studied fisheries in the world. The IPHC is responsible for stock assessments and each year makes its best estimate of the fraction of the halibut population that may be safely and sustainably caught. Each country is then responsible for domestic allocation among commercial, sport, and aboriginal groups. The fishery is closed during spawning season, allowing for regeneration of the species.

In 1990, the Individual Transferrable Quota (ITQ) licensing system was implemented. The ITQ system enables vessel owners to catch a certain quota of fish within an eight-month season. Some people feel this system has prevented an oversupply of the market as well as helped fishermen avoid the dangers of "derby" type openings, making it a safe and economically healthy fishery. In order to deter large companies from hoarding the valuable halibut quota, there is a ceiling on how much any one individual can own or lease. In the 2000 fishing season, for example, no one person is permitted to own or lease

over 106,000 pounds of halibut.

Halibut stocks are at near optimal levels, but declining slightly. It is unclear if this is a result of loss of habitat, overfishing, or oceanic conditions. Nonetheless, it means that we need to continue monitoring the fishery and reduce the total allowable catch if the stocks continue to decline.

One particular problem in the halibut long line fishery is its impact on the albatross. These magnificent seabirds dive for the bait on long line hooks and get

CONSERVATION TIPS

1 Ask your local fish market to purchase only halibut that has been caught outside of albatross areas or that has been caught with bird-deterrent devices.

2 Look for our yearly updates of which fish are okay to purchase. We will let you know if the stocks are declining and further actions need to be taken.

3 Write a letter to the Canadian Minister of Fisheries and Oceans or the government agency near you urging the establishment of a network of marine protected areas with a core of no-take zones. (See sample letter in the Appendix.)

caught, dragging them slowly to the bottom of the ocean to their death. As a result, albatross populations have dropped drastically in past years; however, steps have been taken to reduce this problem and albatross numbers are again on the rise.

Most of the critical albatross habitat is in Alaska, where procedures have been implemented to eliminate any albatross bycatch. It is mandatory that all fishermen use bird-deterrent devices, which are designed to scare the albatross away from the baited hooks. There are about five different devices which have been developed by fishermen, all of which are inexpensive and easy to use. According to Alaskan Fisheries managers, if fishermen are discovered to have caught more than four albatross in two years, the Alaskan fishery will be terminated.

In B.C., it is not mandatory to use this gear, although most fishermen who fish in the areas frequented by albatross use it on a voluntary basis. The International Pacific Halibut Commission has claimed that bird-deterrent devices will probably become mandatory in albatross-sensitive areas by 2005. We believe they should be mandatory now.

Another conservation issue in the halibut fishery is the amount of rockfish bycatch. Because halibut are often found in areas inhabited by certain species of rockfish (such as the yelloweye), halibut fishermen accidentally catch rockfish on their long lines. Avoiding the rockfish bycatch is a difficult thing to do without completely closing the fishery. We believe that establishing marine protected areas on the halibut fishing grounds will best protect the rockfish that inhabit the areas, as well as protect vital habitat for spawning halibut. This does not mean that the entire fishing grounds must be off-limits. Instead, we need to work with the commercial fishing fleets to determine which areas would be best for protection.

Finally, there are concerns about the amount of fish being caught by the recreational fishery. As salmon decline, more anglers are fishing for halibut, but the catches often go unrecorded. As a result, we are unsure of how many halibut are taken every year by the recreational fishery, making it difficult to ensure that enough spawners remain in the water.

If you have the opportunity to purchase halibut directly from a fisherman, we highly recommend it. This means that you are not only assured that the fish you buy is the freshest possible, you are also supporting your local fishery. However, according to Health Canada regulations, a fisherman is not allowed to fillet the fish for you. Because fish under thirty-two inches in length cannot be sold at all, when you purchase halibut from a fisherman, you will be taking home one *big* fish. Ask the fisherman to show you how to best fillet a halibut and freeze meal-size portions. Make sure the fillets are well wrapped to avoid freezer burn.

If you are purchasing halibut from a market, the fish should be displayed on ice, and its flesh should be translucent and shiny with no noticeable smell. Do not purchase meat with blotches and yellow tinges (the tell-tale signs of freezer burn) or meat that is milky and opaque, which indicates poor handling.

athleen Pearson of Skidegate, Haida Gwaii, British Columbia is a commissioner of the International Pacific Halibut Commission (IPHC), which jointly manages the Canadian and American Pacific halibut fishery. She has been a deckhand, a United Fishermen and Allied Workers Union representative, and has worked in fish processing facilities. She was elected to the Council of Haida Nations in 1996.

Kathleen's recipe for baked halibut head may appear unusual, but it is in keeping with the theme of sustainable fishing. By utilizing every portion of the fish, you will obtain as much nourishment from each fish as possible, leaving no waste. The halibut head is full of delicious meat; in fact, halibut cheeks are a rare delicacy, similar in taste and texture to scallops. So don't be squeamish—ask your local fishmonger or the fisher himself for some halibut heads and try Kathleen's recipe. We dare you!

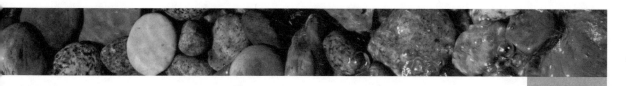

Kathleen Pearson's Baked Halibut Heads

4 halibut heads
4 bacon strips
Salt to taste
Pepper to taste
2 medium onions, thickly sliced

Preheat oven to 350° F. Prepare heads by first removing gills. Clean off all the blood and wash well to remove slime. Cut the mouths off, as there is no meat in this area.

Line a flat cake pan with foil and put halibut heads in it. Place a bacon strip across each head and sprinkle with salt and pepper. Cover pan with foil to keep moisture in. Place in oven and bake for 30 minutes. After 15 minutes baking, add sliced onions on and around the heads. If you like to eat the skin, turn oven to broil near end of cooking time to brown.

Now you are ready to eat a very succulent halibut head. You may want to start with the cheeks. The bony parts (gristle) are very good to suck on, but the eyeballs are an acquired taste!

Russell Cameron's halibut boat Ocean Viking

*R*ussell Cameron lives in Pender Harbour, B.C. with his wife Lynne and his ten-year-old son Samuel. Just like his father and grandfather, Russell was born into the fishing industry and has been involved in many types of fishing. He now spends most of his time at sea fishing for halibut. For the past twenty years, Russell has been a dedicated member of the United Fishermen and Allied Workers Union. He serves as a member of the union's executive board and is president of the local in his area. Russell's wife Lynne found this recipe in the *National Fishermen's Magazine* and it has turned out to be a family favourite.

Photo by Kelly Edwards

The Cameron Family's Halibut Stew

Water
6 large potatoes, cubed
3 carrots, chopped
2 onions, diced
2 stalks green onion, chopped
1 cup white wine
2 lbs. halibut
2 tbsp. butter
2 cloves garlic, crushed
²/₃ cup flour
1¹/₂ cups milk
Salt to taste
Pepper to taste
Dill weed to taste

Stew:

In a large pot full of water, place potatoes, carrots, onions, and green onions and bring to a boil until potatoes are almost cooked. Drain, saving 1¹/₂ cups of liquid. Return liquid back to pot and add wine. This combined liquid should not cover the vegetables. Add the halibut and continue cooking. Remove from heat when halibut has become opaque.

Roux:

A roux will help to thicken the stew. In a saucepan, melt butter over low heat. Add the garlic and sauté, making sure it doesn't turn brown. Stir in flour and let cook for 3 minutes, stirring constantly. Whisk in milk and when thickened, add to stew.

Return to medium heat and stir stew carefully while it thickens. Add salt, pepper, and dill weed to taste.

Makes 4 servings.

$\mathcal{D}$avid Lane is currently the executive director of the T. Buck Suzuki Environmental Foundation, a division of the United Fishermen and Allied Workers Union that speaks out strongly on laws to protect fish habitat. David loves to cook, and the following is one of many of his fine recipes. He says it's great served on a warm summer evening.

Photo by Kelly Edwards

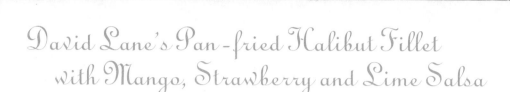

David Lane's Pan-fried Halibut Fillet with Mango, Strawberry and Lime Salsa

1½ lbs. halibut fillet, skin on
2 tbsp. lime juice
2 garlic cloves, minced
2 tbsp. olive oil
Salt to taste
Fresh ground pepper to taste
Fresh parsley, chopped (garnish)

Salsa:
¾ cup fresh strawberries, diced
1 fresh mango, peeled, seeded, and diced
¼ cup red onion, finely diced
⅛ cup red pepper, finely diced
Juice and zest of 1 lime
1 tbsp. olive oil
1 tbsp. cider vinegar
¼ cup fresh cilantro, chopped
Dash of cayenne to taste

Marinate halibut with lime juice, minced garlic, and 1 tablespoon of oil. Set aside.

Chop salsa ingredients, stir well in a small bowl, and refrigerate. In a frying pan on medium heat, pan-fry halibut flesh-side down in remaining oil for 3–5 minutes (depending on thickness of fillet). Turn over and cook for another 5 minutes, until halibut just flakes with a fork. (Broiled or barbecued is also great.)

Serve immediately with a generous portion of salsa on the side or on top.

Makes 4 servings.

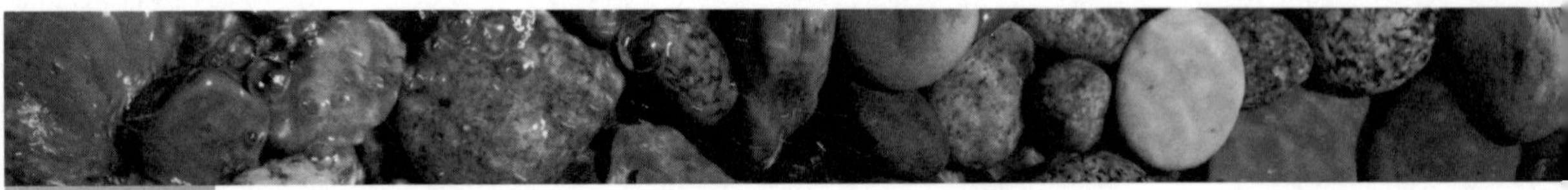

atalie MacMaster, who began to play the fiddle at the age of nine, is now an internationally known performer. She credits her passion for music to her family roots in Cape Breton, Nova Scotia, including her uncle Buddy, a famous fiddler in his own right. Natalie still enjoys playing a reel at the kitchen table, but spends most of her time in recording studios or on stages all over the world. Her busy life leaves her little time for cooking, but this quick and easy recipe for halibut is one that even she can find time to cook!

Natalie MacMaster's Halibut Steaks

4 halibut steaks
2 medium onions, sliced
1 cup lemon juice
Dash of Tabasco sauce
8 slices bacon
2 tbsp. parsley, chopped
Dash of paprika

Preheat oven to 375° F. Lightly grease a large sheet of aluminum foil. Place halibut steaks on foil and surround with onions. Sprinkle steaks with lemon juice and Tabasco sauce. Place bacon slices on top and cover with parsley and paprika. Cover with foil securely and place in oven for 25 to 30 minutes. At end of cooking time, open top of foil and place under broiler to brown the bacon before serving.

Makes 4 servings.

Lingcod

LINGCOD

Lingcod is a delicious white fish with a subtle flavour that melts in your mouth. Its mild taste and texture makes it excellent served with a variety of sauces. This, combined with its impressive size, has been attracting sport and commercial fishermen for many years on the coast of B.C.

Lingcod is actually not a cod at all but a member of the greenling family. They can weigh up to eighty pounds and grow up to five feet in length. Beige in colour with clusters of light brown spots, they have large heads with numerous teeth. Lingcod are voracious eaters and are said to eat constantly, devouring almost any fish or octopus in their vicinity. Found along the west coast, from Alaska to the Baja Peninsula of Mexico, lingcod can also occur over a wide range of depths, from ten to 1,300 feet, but they mostly inhabit rocky areas from thirty to 330 feet in depth. Their natural predators include seals and sea lions.

It is thought that lingcod can live to be as old as seventeen years. Females become sexually mature around the age of four or five, while males sexually mature after two years. The female lingcod lays a nest

LINGCOD STOCKS ARE HEALTHY IN MOST AREAS OF B.C., BUT SEVERELY DEPLETED IN THE STRAIT OF GEORGIA.

of eggs that can weigh as much as thirty pounds and have anywhere from 60,000 to 500,000 eggs. The size of the egg mass depends on the size of the fish; larger and older females tend to lay more eggs. Once the eggs are fertilized, the female moves into deeper water and the males remain to guard and fan the eggs until they hatch. These large male fish are quite aggressive in their efforts to protect the eggs and will charge anything they perceive as a threat. Curious scuba divers have been know to have lingcod swim right up to their masks to try to scare them away! It is best to leave them to do their jobs in peace.

Because they are relatively long-lived, slow to mature, and non-migratory, lingcod populations are easily affected by overfishing. Lingcod stocks in the Strait of Georgia, where commercial and recreational harvesting has occurred the longest, are currently ninety-one percent lower than they were in 1889. This dramatic decline has resulted in the closing of the commercial lingcod fishery in most areas of the Strait of Georgia, a predicament that must be avoided elsewhere on the west coast. In order to ensure a sustainable fishery, we must take steps to rebuild depleted stocks and prevent further depletion of northern stocks where fishing still takes place.

There are two different types of fishing techniques in the commercial lingcod fishery: trawling and trolling. Trawlers catch seventy-four percent of the total allowable catch while trollers catch the remaining twenty-six percent. Bottom trawling in hard habitat causes more habitat disruption to our seedbeds then any other form of harvest. Dragging heavy nets and gear over the ocean bottom destroys bottom-dwelling creatures and the rocky habitat they require. It would be ideal if all trawling on hard bottom habitats could be eventually phased out and replaced with less harmful methods.

The recreational fishery for lingcod is growing every year. The decline in opportunities for sport salmon fishing along with the huge physical size of the lingcod makes them highly desirable. However, the poor reporting of the lingcod recreational fishery makes it difficult to know exactly how many are being caught. In addition, sport fishermen are allowed to catch lingcod all year round.

Marine protected areas can play a vital role in rebuilding depleted stocks. By protecting lingcod habitat and nesting grounds, we can ensure a healthy spawning population that will help rebuild the lingcod stocks. In fact, it was the crash of the lingcod and rockfish stocks that inspired local residents and divers to establish the Whytecliff Park and Porteau Cove marine protected areas in the Howe Sound Region.

The Annual Lingcod Egg Mass Survey, co-ordinated by the Vancouver Aquarium Marine Science Centre, has demonstrated the effectiveness of marine protected areas in the protection of lingcod nesting grounds. During peak spawning time in February, recreational divers count lingcod egg nests and assess their size, recording the information and sending it to the Vancouver Aquarium for processing. This survey, underway since 1995, shows that the number and size of egg nests in the marine protected areas is higher than

CONSERVATION TIPS

1 We recommend that you don't buy any fresh lingcod during the spawning season, from the middle of November through the middle of April. This will ensure that the lingcod you eat are not harvested from their nests.

2 When purchasing lingcod, ask for troll-caught fish. When possible, try to buy directly from fishermen.

3 Recreational fishermen should not fish for lingcod in the Strait of Georgia at all.

areas where fishing occurs. This suggests that establishing marine protected areas can contribute substantially to the rebuilding of our fish stocks.

Establishing marine protected areas can also help prevent overfishing, and by protecting spawning areas we can ensure that stocks are being replenished as much as possible. Establishing marine protected areas is different from just closing the fishery during spawning time. Well-planned, permanent marine protected areas, along with seasonal spawning closures, will together protect nesting areas and spawning lingcod.. MPAs will also protect the habitat from bottom trawling, dumping, and dredging, thereby ensuring the fish have nesting grounds to return to.

We also need to ensure that the lingcod stocks are left alone during the spawning season; thus, we advocate no lingcod harvesting in B.C. waters from November 15 to April 15. This already applies in the south coast, but it would be better if the ban were implemented along the entire coast.

When purchasing lingcod, the flesh should be white, sometimes with a slight blue or green tinge; it will turn pure white, with a smooth yet firm texture, when cooked. Lingcod are marketed either fresh or frozen as fillets or steaks. Shelf life is five to seven days at 40° F. You can keep them frozen for six to nine months.

*J*ennifer Lash is the founder and Executive Director of Living Oceans Society, a conservation organization based in Sointula, B.C. Jennifer fell in love with the ocean and its many creatures when she began diving in 1989. Since then she has been adventuring underwater in Australia, the Caribbean, and many parts of British Columbia. As a conservationist, Jennifer is concerned about the people who live in coastal communities. Consequently, Living Oceans Society is committed to finding ways to promote ecological and economic sustainability. It was during her outreach work with commercial fishermen that she met and married Bruce Burrows, a long-time commercial fisherman. Bruce and Jennifer are the parents of newly-born twins, Molly and Dexter, born August 4, 2000. Jennifer says this lingcod salad makes a wonderful appetizer or a full meal when served with bread and cheese. The sauce is very rich and the recipes can be adjusted to your taste.

Jennifer Lash's Warm Lingcod Salad

1 head romaine lettuce
¼ cup almonds, sliced
1 medium carrot, julienned
Splash of olive oil

¾ lb. lingcod fillets, cubed
½ cup mayonnaise
½ cup sour cream
2 tbsp. soy sauce

Wash and pat dry lettuce leaves. Tear into bite-sized pieces and place in a large non-metal bowl. Lightly toast almonds in a frying pan and set aside. In the same pan, sauté julienned carrots in olive oil until tender. Add lingcod meat and continuing sautéing until meat is cooked through and tender. Be careful not to overcook. Add mayonnaise, sour cream, and soy sauce to pan and simmer over low heat until sauce is hot.

In a large serving bowl, place lingcod and sauce over lettuce leaves and toss well. Add toasted almonds and serve immediately.

Makes 4 servings.

Photo by Alexandra Morton

$\mathcal{B}$illy Proctor is a true resident of the B.C. coast. Born on remote Swanson Island in the Broughton Archipelago, he lost his father in a fishing accident when he was only seven years old. His mother remained in the area running a fish camp until her death many years later. Bill grew up with very little means of communication with the outside world and he avoids city life to this day.

Since his youth, Billy has lived in different parts of the Broughton Archipelago, settling finally in the community of Echo Bay on Gilford Island. He and his wife Yvonne have a homestead where they raised their children and where they now have a museum of artifacts Billy has collected over the years. Billy has earned a living from both the forest (logging) and from the sea (fishing), and has witnessed changes in both industries, doing what he can to come to their aid. He has spoken out against fish farms, been involved in protests against the restructuring of the salmon fleet, was a founder of the Scott Cove Fish Hatchery, and is currently trying to protect the Ahta River from logging.

Billy has been a lingcod fisherman since 1988, and over the years he has watched the number of boats fishing his favourite spots increase. He believes that changes need to be made to ensure that he and other small boat fishermen will always have a place in this fishery.

Billy Proctor's Deep Fried Lingcod

Canola oil (enough for deep fryer)
3 lbs. lingcod fillets, cubed

Batter:
1 cup flour
1 tsp. salt
1 tsp. baking powder
¼ tsp. baking soda
¼ tsp. black pepper
Water
1 tsp. vinegar

In a deep fryer, heat the canola oil until bubbling. Cut lingcod into cubes 1 inch by 2 inches and pat dry. Stir the dry ingredients together and add enough cold water to make a thick batter. Just before using, add vinegar, then dip fish into batter and then carefully place into fryer. Cook in bubbling oil in fryer until golden brown.

Makes 4 servings.

*a*s mentioned in the chapter on clams, Don Genova is the host of *Pacific Palate* and *Food for Thought* on CBC Radio, writes a column called "Pacific Palate" for MyBC.com, and occasionally contributes to the *National Post, Homes West,* and *BC Business Magazine.*

Don Genova's East Indian Fish Stew

1 lb. lingcod fillets, cubed
1 2-inch piece of fresh ginger, peeled and chopped
8 cloves garlic, peeled
½ cup almonds, slivered and blanched
2–4 tbsp. water
2 tbsp. vegetable oil
2 medium onions, chopped
1 tsp. cumin
1 tsp. cardamon
1 tsp. cinnamon

1 tsp. ground coriander
2 cups chicken stock or water
1 28-oz. can of tomatoes, puréed with the juice
½ cup red lentils
2 small potatoes, peeled and diced small
1 14-oz. can chickpeas
Salt to taste
Pepper to taste
½ cup cilantro, chopped (garnish)

Cut lingcod fillets into bite-sized pieces and set aside. In a blender or food processor, purée ginger, garlic, almonds, and water. In a medium pot, sauté onions in vegetable oil until translucent, then add spices and stir. Add almond mixture and stir again. Be careful spices don't stick to the bottom of the pot. Pour in water or chicken stock and the puréed tomatoes, and bring to a boil. Reduce to a simmer and add lentils and potatoes. Simmer until potatoes are cooked, then add chickpeas and the fish, which should only take a few moments to cook through. Season to taste, and serve in bowls topped with the fresh cilantro.

Makes 6–8 servings.

Octopus

OCTOPUS

When most people think of octopus they don't think of it as a food source, but octopus has become an exciting food product for more adventurous diners. Preparation is the secret to its success. Its meat is naturally tough, but when tenderized it becomes a delicious meal. This chapter will provide the secrets to tenderizing and preparing octopus, but first a bit of background on these magnificent creatures.

The most common octopus species in B.C. waters, and the only one that is commercially harvested, is the Pacific Octopus. It is the largest species of octopus in the world, growing as large as thirty feet in diameter with its tentacles spread. They are short-lived creatures, living only three to four years. The male octopus dies soon after it mates, leaving the female to guard the nest. The female lays her eggs and puts all her energy into protecting them for the following five to six months. Once the eggs hatch, she will also die.

One of the most fascinating aspects of the octopus is how it protects itself from predators. By releasing a black fluid from its ink gland, it creates a cloud of dark, inky water that confuses predators and gives the octopus a chance to escape. The ink is thought to anaesthetize the sensory system of predators, particularly fish.

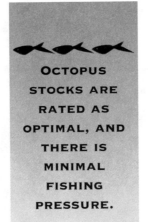

OCTOPUS STOCKS ARE RATED AS OPTIMAL, AND THERE IS MINIMAL FISHING PRESSURE.

Another amazing characteristic is its ability to change colour to match its environment. Its skin contains pigment cells, called chromatophores, made up of several colours, including yellow, orange, red, blue, and black. By expanding and contracting different pigment cells, the octopus can change its appearance to blend in with its environment and thus become invisible to predators.

Historically there have been two major markets for octopus: the domestic bait fishery, and export to Japan. The Japanese demand for octopus is quite high, especially since they have completely over-harvested their own stocks. The experience in Japan is a reminder that octopus can be overfished, and although our stocks are healthy right now, we must take steps to ensure that this situation continues. The bait fishery used to supply octopus to other commercial fisheries; however, bait sales have declined in past years.

Since 1996, there has been a growing interest in developing a local commercial food fishery for octopus. The increased interest has led the Canadian Department of Fisheries and Oceans to change to more sustainable fishing techniques. Diving is the main method of harvesting octopus. In the past, divers used bleach to force octopus out of their dens; however, this was banned in 2000. Fishermen are now experimenting with more benign methods such as using lemon juice and vinegar. These solutions are less effective than bleach, but much gentler on the ocean. In addition, divers must track the number of octopus they catch, as well as where they catch them.

Octopus can be purchased at select seafood markets. While octopus may look intimidating, the delectable recipes included here will encourage you to give it a try.

1 Look for our yearly updates of which fish are okay to purchase. We will let you know if the stocks are declining and whether further action needs to be taken.

$\mathcal{P}$eter Brown, his wife Charmaine, and their four children live in Metchosin, B.C. Peter has been fishing since 1972, starting as a salmon troller and then moving into the dive fisheries. He was active in the abalone and sea cucumber fishery but now focuses mainly on octopus. When diving for octopus, Peter and his crew use a small open skiff to get into shallow areas.

Peter has been searching a long time for the ultimate way to tenderize and prepare octopus. He says the easiest way to tenderize it is to place a bed of coarse salt in a plastic tub, bury the octopus in it for a few days, then remove it and rinse well. Place in smoker for 8–10 hours. After this process, the octopus can be canned, which creates a beautiful product.

Photo by Kelly Edwards

Peter Brown's Superb Octopus Pasta Salad

6 cups cooked pasta (rotini or penne)
2 red apples, chopped
2 cups cheese, shredded (your choice)
8 oz. smoked octopus, chopped
4 stalks green onion, chopped
²/₃ cup mayonnaise
1 tsp. lemon juice
4 lettuce leaves (optional)

In a large bowl, place all the ingredients and toss well. Refrigerate until ready to serve. Serve on a bed of lettuce if desired.

Makes 4 servings.

C is one of Vancouver's leading restaurants, both in the quality of its food and its commitment to use only sustainably caught seafood products. By selling only products it deems as sustainable and buying local products as much as possible, this restaurant is taking proactive steps to promote sustainable fisheries in B.C. In addition, C is not shy about sharing its commitment with its patrons, spreading the word that consumers can play an active role in ensuring fresh seafood will be available for generations to come. Their recipes for sustainable products such as octopus demonstrate the inspiration and creativity of its chefs; each dish is uniquely prepared, combining the influences of Asian, French, and West Coast cuisine with tantalizing results.

The following is a method C chef Robert Clark has developed for preparing its famous octopus bacon.

Photo by Kelly Edwards

C's Octopus Bacon

2 lbs. pickling salt
12 lbs. octopus
8 oz. coarse kosher salt
4 oz. sugar
32 oz. water
Canola oil (as needed)

Using ⅓ of the pickling salt as an abrasive, scrub octopus to remove slime. Rinse and repeat this step three times, using up all the pickling salt. Rinse well and place in a non-reactive container (a crock pot works well). Cover with mixture of kosher salt, water, and sugar. Soak in this brine for 14 to 18 hours.

In a warm smoker (e.g., Little Chief) using maple chips, smoke octopus for about two hours. When meat is smoked, place in large pot and cover with canola oil. Cook slowly for about 1½ to 2 hours, depending on size of octopus. Let meat cool in oil. When cool enough to handle, drain off oil. Wearing rubber gloves, remove suction cups from tentacles by rubbing your hands down from the head to the tips. Cut into 6–8 inch pieces, then slice. Grill and serve.

C's Octopus Bacon and Barley Broth

2 cups onions, diced
2 cups octopus bacon, chopped
$\frac{1}{5}$ cup oil
1 cup turnip, diced
1 cup celery, diced
1 cup rutabaga, diced
1 cup leeks, diced
2 tbsp. garlic, finely chopped
$\frac{1}{2}$ cup barley, well washed
5 bay leaves
1 tsp. nutmeg, freshly ground
4 litres chicken stock
2 tbsp. fresh thyme, chopped
2 tbsp. fresh parsley, chopped

In a large pot, sweat onions and octopus bacon in the oil. Add all ingredients except chicken stock and fresh herbs, and cook for two minutes. Add the stock and simmer gently until barley is cooked. Remove bay leaves and add the fresh herbs.

Makes 6–8 servings.

Rockfish

ROCKFISH

These white fish, which have graced the tables of most recreational fishermen in B.C., are commonly called cod or rock cod, but rockfish are not related to cod at all and are in fact part of the *Sebastes* genus. There are thirty-four different species of rockfish in B.C. and over 100 different species worldwide. They come in all shapes, sizes, and colours, in a wide array of patterns from spotted to striped, have big eyes and a mouth that gives them the appearance of frowning. Members of an extensive family of fish known as scorpion fish, rockfish have venomous spines on their large dorsal fins.

Rockfish have a long life span, and do not even start reproducing until they are at least ten to twenty years of age, depending on the species. For example, the yellow eye rockfish can live up to 117 years and doesn't start reproducing until the age of twenty. Adult rockfish are also believed to remain on their home reefs, which makes them extremely susceptible to over-harvesting.

Rockfish have been targeted by commercial fisheries since the 1950s. The commercial trawl fishery is currently responsible for catching ninety percent of the

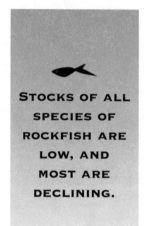

STOCKS OF ALL SPECIES OF ROCKFISH ARE LOW, AND MOST ARE DECLINING.

rockfish in B.C., using mid-water trawls and bottom trawls. The remainder of the rockfish are caught for the live fishery by hook and line (the yellow eye fishery uses long line gear).

Bottom trawling in hard habitat causes more disruption to our seedbed than any other form of harvest. Dragging heavy nets and gear over the bottom of the ocean destroys many of the creatures who dwell there, as well as the rocky habitat they require. It would be ideal if all trawling on hard-bottom habitats could eventually be phased out and replaced with less harmful methods.

Since the 1950s, stocks of rockfish in the Strait of Georgia have been seriously depleted, another indication of the susceptibility of rockfish to over-fishing. At present, the trawl fishery is closed in the Strait of Georgia, although the hook and line fishery remains, despite the declining stocks. It is believed that rockfish stocks throughout the west coast will face the same fate as the Strait of Georgia unless significant steps are taken to change management practices.

Since the late 1980s, the recreational fishery has increased dramatically. In fact, it is believed that the

1999 recreational catches in the Strait of Georgia were equal to that of the commercial fishery. Many fishermen, hoping to limit the impact on the fish stocks, practice the technique of catch and release. However, rockfish rarely survive after being caught and released. They have an organ called a swim bladder that makes it possible for them to control their buoyancy, thus preventing them from floating to the top or sinking to the bottom. This organ makes the rockfish vulnerable to rapid changes in pressure, such as being pulled to the surface by a fishing rod. As the fish is brought to the surface, the air inside the swim bladder expands and can fatally damage the internal organs of the fish. Although it may appear that the fish are healthy, it is believed that many of them eventually die as a result of being caught. Therefore, the catch and release efforts of recreational fishermen do not help to conserve fish stocks. This is also a problem in the commercial fisheries, where rockfish bycatch cannot be released because of damage caused to their internal organs.

As a result, the Canadian Department of Fisheries and Oceans recommends that when fishing recreationally, all rockfish should be retained, regardless of size. The general rule of thumb recommended by DFO is to keep what you catch and avoid rockfish if you attain the daily limit. However, we recommend that recreational fishermen avoid catching rockfish altogether.

Rockfish are prime candidates to benefit from the establishment of marine protected areas. By protecting nursery grounds and healthy spawning stock, we believe that rockfish populations can rebuild, thereby creating a sustainable fishery. This has already been

CONSERVATION TIPS

1 Write a letter to the Canadian Department of Fisheries and Oceans (or the government agency in your area) stating that you will support the rockfish fishery when a network of marine protected areas has been established. (See sample letter in the Appendix.)

2 Don't target rockfish when recreational fishing. If you accidentally catch a rockfish, do not let it go, as it will not survive. Report it as a harvested fish and take it home for dinner.

3 There is a heavy demand for live one- to three-pound rockfish. Consequently, other fish that are caught but not purchased are wasted. When purchasing rockfish, take what you can get in terms of size. This will ensure that all the fish that are caught are used, eliminating waste.

proven in the Edmunds Underwater Preserve in central Puget Sound. Closed to fishing for twenty-five years, this area is now home to large numbers of rockfish that produce a significant number of larvae every year. Research has shown larger rockfish stocks within several miles of the reserve, but elsewhere in Puget Sound, they are drastically lower.

Living Oceans Society believes that setting up a network of marine protected areas where recreational and commercial fishing is prohibited will allow for the rebuilding of rockfish populations and the development of sustainable fisheries.

Don Genova's East Indian Fish Stew (pg. 60)

Gordie Sampson's Shrimp Curry (pg. 98)

James Barber's Fried Shrimp and Mango Salad (pg. 93)

Will and Heidi Soltou's Barbecued Salmon with Spring Vegetables (pg. 109)

Sooke Harbour House's Crab Consommé (pg. 129)

im Stockwood is a Newfoundland-born singer who came on to the Canadian music scene in 1995 with her debut release *Bona Vista*. Reaching gold-level sales in Canada, it produced four highly charted singles. This extroverted, fun-loving woman continues to dazzle as a person and as an artist. Her sensitive and thoughtful side comes out in her recent release *12 Years Old*. The following is her yummy cod recipe.

Photo by Tim Morrison

Kim Stockwood's Cod au Gratin

1 2-lb. rockfish, flaked
$^1\!/_2$ cup butter
$^1\!/_2$ cup flour
2 $^1\!/_2$ cups milk
1 small onion, chopped
2 tsp. salt
2 tsp. pepper
1 cup cheddar cheese, grated
1 cup breadcrumbs

Preheat oven to 375° F. Place rockfish in greased baking dish or individual baking dishes. In a saucepan, melt butter, then stir in flour until smooth. Remove from heat. Gradually stir in half of milk, return to heat, and stir until smooth. Slowly add remaining milk, salt, pepper, and onions. Continue stirring until smooth and thickened. Pour sauce over fish and top with cheese and breadcrumbs. Cook for 20 to 25 minutes until sauce bubbles and fish is cooked.

Makes 4 servings.

*J*on Taylor is a rockfish fisherman and a resident of Sointula, B.C. He spends many a day on his forty-foot wooden troller, the *Open Sea*, enjoying the ocean life. Although he makes his living harvesting rockfish, Jon believes that some areas should be off limits to commercial and recreational fishermen. By protecting healthy rockfish nurseries, Jon feels that his fishery can improve and become more sustainable. Critical to the success of these protected areas is prohibiting all commercial and recreational fishing. Here is Jon's recipe for baked rockfish using a whole fish.

Photo by Kelly Edwards

Jon Taylor's Baked Rockfish

Rockfish can be hard to handle because of the spines. Jon recommends keeping them in the freezer until you are ready to use them.

1 whole rockfish (if using small rockfish, prepare one per person)
Pickling salt

Preheat oven to 350° F. Line roasting pan with a ¹⁄₂-inch layer of pickling salt. Take fish out of freezer and scrape scales off with a knife. Pat fish with pickling salt and place it (still frozen) in roasting pan on top of a layer of salt. Bake in oven for 30 to 45 minutes. Peel away skin and meat and enjoy.

Makes approximately 4 servings.

Jon Taylor's Rockfish Stew

The best part of this recipe is its simplicity. Jon makes this often when he is out fishing, because it works well on the oil stove and is quick and easy, as well as warm and hearty. The simple ingredients makes it particularly good for boating trips.

1 large onion, cubed
2 large potatoes, cubed
1 rockfish, filleted and cubed
Canned milk (canned milk is an important standby for fishermen as fresh milk is not always available, and its thick, rich quality contributes to the finished product)
Salt to taste
Pepper to taste

In a large pot, add cubed onions and potatoes and cover with water. Bring to a boil, then simmer until potatoes are tender. Remove from heat and add fish, salt, pepper, and canned milk to taste. Slide pot to cool part of stove and go out on deck and check your lines; when you are done, it should be ready.

Makes 4 servings.

Umberto Menghi started out his life on a typical Tuscan farm in Pontedara, Tuscany. His parents had high hopes of him becoming a priest, but at the age of twelve, the pressure became too much and he ran away from home. He was taken in by a couple who owned a restaurant and he helped them out with various restaurant chores. When his father came to retrieve him, he informed him he was going to stay. It was at this time that Umberto realized that the restaurant business was his calling in life. He went on to attend a college for hotel management in Rome and it was there he gained the skills that guaranteed his success in the hospitality business. In 1973, he opened his first restaurant, Umberto's, in Vancouver. Since then he has opened other restaurants, and in 1995 started the Villa Delia Cooking School in Tuscany. His love for the business, the pleasure of entertaining people, and his passion for food itself is reflected in everything he does.

Umberto Menghi's Poached Fillet of Rockfish with Orange Sauce

4 6–8-oz. fillets fresh rockfish
Salt to taste
Pepper to taste
Juice of 2 oranges
$\frac{1}{2}$ cup dry white wine
$\frac{1}{4}$ cream
2 tbsp. butter
8 sections of orange, peeled and seeded (garnish)
Zest of $\frac{1}{2}$ an orange, blanched (drop zest in boiling water for 30 seconds)
  (garnish)

Rinse rockfish fillets under cold running water and pat dry with paper towels. Season with salt and pepper and place in a buttered baking dish. Preheat oven to 350° F. Pour orange juice over fillets and sprinkle with pepper. Add white wine to baking dish. Cover the baking dish with a sheet of buttered paper. Place dish in oven and poach for 8–10 minutes, then remove from oven, place fillets on a platter, set aside, and keep warm. Reserve liquid in dish and transfer to saucepan from heat. Add cream to saucepan, blend, and simmer for approximately 1 minute, then remove saucepan from heat. Add butter to saucepan and blend. Season with salt and pepper. Spoon contents of saucepan over fillets of rockfish on platter. Garnish each fillet with two sections of orange and sprinkled orange zest. Serve immediately.

Makes 4 servings.

Sablefish

SABLEFISH (BLACK COD)

*I*f you are looking for a rich, smoky kind of fish, then sablefish will fit the bill. Flavourful and unique, this fish is a nice change from the usual salmon and halibut. It has been known as black cod to coastal residents for generations, but recently underwent a name change to the more refined "sablefish," primarily for marketing purposes. But either name will get you the same delicious fish for dinner.

Sablefish can be found in widely-ranging areas, from Baja California to Japan and the Bering Sea. Large groups of them are commonly found in waters off northern B.C. and the Gulf of Alaska. Sablefish spawn from January to March along the continental shelf at depths of 900 to 1,300 feet.

Larval sablefish are found in shallow waters over the shelf and slope in April and May. Juveniles move inshore over the following six months and grow up in near-shore and shelf areas until three to five years of age, when they migrate offshore and into depths greater than 5,000 feet. A good example of this is the movement of juveniles from nursing grounds in Hecate Strait in B.C. to the Gulf of Alaska and the Bering Sea. Sablefish grow rapidly, and reach sexual maturity at about four or five years. The average

adult size is twenty-one inches, although the largest recorded fish was 31.5 inches and was estimated to be 113 years old.

Sablefish have been harvested off the west coast of B.C. for more than forty years. Originally, sablefish were caught as a bycatch in long line and trawl fisheries and were not specifically targeted. In the late 1970s, Canadian fishermen worked to establish a viable sablefish fishery by pursuing markets in Japan and experimenting with trap gear as a more effective and productive harvesting method. In 1981, their efforts began to pay off as market demand increased.

Although sablefish stocks are near optimal levels, there are a few problems with the way the fishery in B.C. is structured. The primary concern is the use of an Individual Transferable Quota (ITQ) licensing system. ITQ licenses mean that anyone can purchase one of the forty-eight licenses available and hire people to work on their boat. Although this system can make it easier to manage the fishery, it often results in corporate ownership of the licenses. Furthermore, it allows for an unfair concentration of the licenses, meaning the same amount of fish is being caught but fewer jobs are

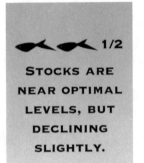

1/2

STOCKS ARE NEAR OPTIMAL LEVELS, BUT DECLINING SLIGHTLY.

created; in 1993, the forty-eight ITQ sablefish licenses issued went to only twenty-six boats.

Transferable quotas are bought and sold at prices too high for a small-scale boat owner to afford. In New Zealand, four major companies control the majority of both inshore and deep water fishing quotas. In Greymouth, a small coastal village, ninety percent of the fishermen are fishing for company-owned quota and are forced to accept whatever price the company offers. This has drastically altered New Zealand's coastal lifestyle.

History has proven that the best managers of the fish stocks are the people with a vested interest in its long-term sustainability. Many fisheries around the world were sustainable for generations until large corporate fleets moved in. Corporations often do not have a long-term commitment and will advocate higher yearly catches to increase profits, which is not always in the best interest of the health of the fish stocks.

A better management scheme would be owner-operator-based, in which the person who owns the license must actually work on the boat. By maintaining the connection between economic benefits and the health of the fish stocks, we can ensure that fishermen become guardians of the fish while making their living. This would help to prevent corporate takeovers such as the one in New Zealand.

The second issue of concern with the sablefish fishery is the different types of gear used. Most boats use trap gear, which virtually eliminates rockfish bycatch. However, some of the smaller boats continue to use the long lines, which do have a bycatch problem. Although we feel that trap gear should be mandatory, for economic reasons it is often the small owner-operated boats that continue to use long lines. It is our belief that the Canadian Department of Fisheries and Oceans must provide financial assistance to allow owner-operators to switch to the more beneficial trap gear.

Meanwhile, the Canadian Sablefish Association is working to increase awareness of this great fish product. Although only originally available in smoked form, more and more places are now selling fresh sablefish. Purchasing either smoked or fresh sablefish will definitely add to your seafood repertoire. We hope the recipes that follow will encourage you to try this fish.

1 Look for our yearly updates of which fish are okay to purchase. We will let you know if the stocks are declining and whether further action needs to be taken.

ilf Philips of Pender Harbour, B.C., grew up in the fishing industry. By the age of sixteen, Wilf owned and operated his own gillnetter. After high school, Wilf fished part-time while studying marine biology at Simon Fraser University in Burnaby, B.C. After six years of trying to earn his degree while remaining in the fishing industry, his love for the fishing life won out and Wilf returned to fishing full-time. While long lining for halibut, Wilf applies his black cod bycatch to his black cod license, and fishes the remainder of his catch with traps. This is a perfect way for fishermen to handle their bycatch issues, but unfortunately, most fishermen cannot afford several licenses. The following recipe is a delicious, Asian-influenced way to cook sablefish.

Wilf Philips' Sablefish Stir Fry

2–3 lbs. sablefish, cubed
$^1/_2$ cup light teriyaki sauce
Juice of $^1/_2$ lemon
2 tbsp. olive oil
2 cups broccoli, chopped
1 cup snow peas or frozen peas
2 cups mushrooms

$^1/_2$ medium onion, finely sliced
1 red pepper, chopped
1 green pepper, chopped
1 cup cauliflower
$^1/_2$ cup cashews or almond slices
2 cups cooked rice

Marinate the sablefish in teriyaki and lemon juice for 1–2 hours. While fish is marinating, cut up vegetables; the choice of vegetables is optional.

In a wok or large frying pan, heat the oil. When wok is hot, add marinated fish, stir, and turn pieces over for 1 minute. Add the vegetables and cashews or almonds and cover for another minute.Add remaining marinade and stir together. When vegetables are tender but still crisp, it is ready. Serve over a bed of rice.

Makes 4–6 servings.

Wilf Philips' Six Steps to Smoking Your Own Sablefish

Although most sablefish you buy is already processed and smoked, creating your own smoked sablefish is economical and can result in a superior product. You can freeze your homemade smoked sablefish for up to six months if you package it properly. It will be worth it! Here is what you need and how to do it:

Step 1: Get a Sablefish
You can sometimes find sablefish at a fish market or, even better, buy it directly from a sablefish fisher. If you live on the west coast, take a walk to the nearby docks and ask around. If this is not an option, ask you local fish market to order some for you.

Step 2: Get a Smoker
Most important is the smoker. While many people living in rural areas on the west coast have homemade backyard smokers, these are rarely found in the city. Fortunately, there are small manufactured smokers available that can fit on your back porch. Check you local hardware or fishing tackle store for different brands.

Step 3: Prepare the Sablefish
Fillet the sablefish but leave the skin on. The following proportions are for one fish (two fillets), so multiply the amounts by how many fish you have.

Step 4: Salting the Sablefish
Mix together:
2 cups coarse salt
2 cups brown sugar
2 tsp. fresh ginger, chopped

Sprinkle the mixture over the bottom of roasting pan or tub (use a container suitable for the amount of fish you are smoking). Lay the fish skin side down, and sprinkle more of the mixture over top of fish. Place another layer of fish over top, and repeat layers until all the fish is used. Let stand for 2 to 2½ hours.

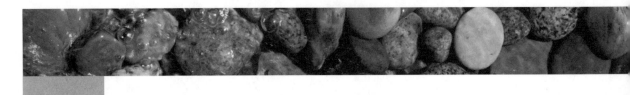

Step 5: Smoking the Sablefish
Rinse the fish and place onto racks of smoker. Smoke lightly for approximately 3 hours or until fish has a light brown colour. When fish is ready, cut into portions and freeze in airtight packages (sealed plastic bags or vacuum packer).

Step 6: Serving Your Home-Smoked Sablefish
Place smoked fish in boiling water or steam it for 10–15 minutes, depending on thickness. Serve with rice and vegetables.

*a*s mentioned in the chapter on octopus, C is one of Vancouver's leading restaurants, both in the quality of its food and its commitment to use only sustainably caught seafood products. Here is C's delectable recipe for grilled sablefish.

C's Grilled Sablefish

32 oz. sablefish (4 8-oz. steaks)

Marinade:
2 tbsp. white wine
1 tbsp. lemon myrtle (a specialty herb in which flavours are brought out by distillation)
Zest from 2 lemons
2 whole shallots, sliced
2 tsp. sesame oil
2 tbsp. vegetable oil
½ tsp. fresh ground pepper

Garnish:
¼ cup red cabbage, shredded
¼ cup carrots, shredded
2 tbsp. rice wine vinegar
1 tbsp. white sesame seeds

Rice:
1 ½ cups short-grained sushi rice
2 cups water
2-inch piece kelp kombu (optional; available in Asian markets)
2 tbsp. seasoned rice wine vinegar

Sauce:
1 tbsp. sesame oil
2 tbsp. vegetable oil
1 tsp. ginger, grated
2 tsp. Dijon mustard

Marinade:

Bring wine to a boil and pour over the lemon myrtle. Let sit for 5 minutes. In a ceramic bowl, add wine, lemon myrtle, lemon zest, shallots, sesame oil, vegetable oil, and freshly ground pepper. Mix with a wire whisk and pour over the four pieces of sablefish, coating them completely. Let stand for 2 hours.

Garnish:

Grate red cabbage and carrots, then mix with rice wine vinegar and sesame seeds. Let stand for 1 hour.

Rice:

If you have a rice cooker, place the washed rice, water, and the optional kelp in the cooker and turn it on. If not, place the washed rice, water, and kelp into a stainless steel pot and bring to a boil on high heat. Remove kelp, cover lightly, and boil for 1 minute. Turn the heat down to medium and cook for 3 or more minutes. Turn heat down to very low and cook for about 10 minutes or until the water is absorbed. Turn heat off and keep covered for another 10 minutes.

Sauce:

Whisk all sauce ingredients together.

All items can be served together at room temperature, so have plates ready next to your grill. Drain marinade off fish so it does not drip into the grill. When grill is cleaned, hot, and well-oiled, place sablefish on grill, turning once, being careful not to overcook it; it is wonderfully flaky when just underdone. Remove from the grill directly to plates, add sauce and garnish, and serve with the rice.

Makes 4 servings.

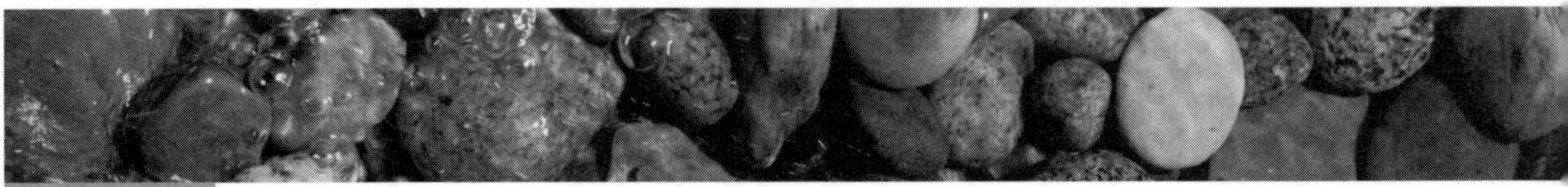

As mentioned in the chapter on crabs, Karen Barnaby is chef at The Fish House in Stanley Park in Vancouver, one of the city's top seafood restaurants. Karen says, "Sablefish has been one of my favourite fish since moving to the west coast. I was so impressed with it that I couldn't believe that it was not widely eaten except in the Asian community. Happily, that is slowly changing. I have come up with many different preparations for it including an *osso buco*-style dish and curing it like corned beef. This particular preparation is Japanese-influenced and the Waldorf salad provides the perfect foil to the rich and succulent texture of the sablefish."

Karen Barnaby's Miso Sablefish with Waldorf Salad

³/₄ **cup white miso**
¹/₂ **cup sugar**
¹/₄ **cup sake**
6 tbsp. mirin (a sweet golden wine made from rice; available in Asian markets)
4 6-oz. sablefish fillets, skin on

Mayonnaise:
3 egg yolks
2 tsp. lemon juice
¹/₄ **tsp. salt**
1 tsp. Japanese prepared or 2 tsp. Dijon mustard
1 cup vegetable oil
3 tbsp. white miso
Sprinkle of white pepper
¹/₄ **tsp. grated lemon peel**

Waldorf salad:
2 cups Fuji, or other flavourful apple, cored and cut into ¼-inch dice
¼ cup celery hearts, cut into ¼-inch dice
½ cup daikon radish, peeled and cut into ¼-inch dice (available at Asian markets)
2 stalks green onion, thinly sliced
2 tbsp. pine nuts, toasted
2 tsp. black sesame seeds, toasted

In the top of a double boiler, combine miso, sake, sugar, and mirin. Cook for ½ hour, stirring frequently. Remove from heat and let cool. Coat sablefish with miso mixture. Cover and refrigerate overnight or up to 3 days.

In a food processor, make the mayonnaise. Combine egg yolks, lemon juice, salt, and mustard. With the motor running, pour in oil in a slow, steady stream. When the mayonnaise has emulsified, add miso, pepper, and lemon peel. Pulse to combine. Cover and refrigerate until needed.

When you are ready to serve the cod, make the salad. Combine apple, celery, daikon, green onion, pine nuts, and sesame seeds. Add ½ cup of mayonnaise. Mix well and refrigerate.

Position the oven rack approximately 8 inches under the broiler. Preheat the broiler to high. Place cod skin side up on a baking tray and broil until browned and crisp around the edges, about 5 minutes. Turn over and broil 5 minutes longer. Serve immediately with the Waldorf salad on the side.

Makes 4 servings.

Shrimp

SHRIMP

Fresh shrimp is a treat for all to enjoy and a constant at most fish markets. It usually originates from one of two places: farms in Asia, or the ocean off the west coast. When purchasing shrimp, it is important to select from a fishery that is socially and environmentally responsible.

People often think that the terms "prawn" and "shrimp" are interchangeable, but this is not entirely true, and is a source of some confusion. Prawns are the largest species of shrimp in B.C., and in the wild, generally live in deep, rocky areas. Other shrimp species prefer soft, bottom areas, and most are caught by bottom-trawlers, while prawns are caught with traps.

One-third of the shrimp consumed globally are farmed, with eighty percent of these farms located in Asia. However, this number is much higher in B.C., where approximately eighty-five percent of the shrimp consumed comes from farms overseas. Some have referred to Asia's shrimp industry as the "deadly cash crop" because these shrimp farms consume coastlines and rob fishing locals of their traditional lifestyles. For example, the

CURRENTLY, THE STATUS OF THE STOCKS IS UNKNOWN BUT BELIEVED TO BE HEALTHY.

community of Andhra Pradesh, India has a coastline that has proven enticing for shrimp farmers. Of its 150,000 hectares, 50,000 are currently being used for shrimp production, with more in the works. The shrimp farms provide no benefit to locals, as the shrimp are far too expensive for the natives of these communities to afford, and all of the product is exported to wealthier countries.

The shrimp farms have poisoned the local water supplies with chemicals and high salt levels, leaving the water undrinkable; those who do drink it suffer from horrible skin diseases. Tankers distribute water to people living in the coastal villages, who are rationed two buckets per day. The chemicals that have poisoned the drinking water have also wiped out species of fish and denied villagers access to the sea. The shrimp farmers have shown a lack of respect for both the coastal communities and the environment, and have caused locals to lose their livelihood, traditions, and identities.

In response, the coastal residents organized marches, protests, and peaceful demonstrations against the shrimp farms. Local groups worked hard to show their opposition, but the government refused to take action. They are still fighting to this day, with little progress. As a consumer, you can help these coastal communities by refusing to purchase shrimp that has been farmed.

There are no shrimp farms in B.C.; instead, we have a wild shrimp fishery. The wild shrimp begin their life as larvae that hatch in early spring and settle into shallow areas of water. At around two years of age, they return to the adult grounds. At this point, they are mature and function as adult males, but within six months they begin to transform into females. By the age of three years, shrimp have transformed totally from male into female and are ready to produce eggs.

B.C.'s commercial shrimp fishery has grown incredibly. From 1989 to 1994, there were only six vessels that trawled strictly for shrimp. But due to the many problems faced in other commercial fisheries, by 1997 sixty-five of B.C.'s 248 shrimp fishing boats were dedicated exclusively to fishing for shrimp. The prawn fishery has also grown over the years. A large percentage of both prawn and shrimp license holders live in small coastal communities and make an important contribution to their local economies.

With the growth of B.C.'s shrimp fleet comes the growth of conservation issues surrounding the fishery. The two main concerns with the shrimp trawl fishery are the amount of bycatch and the impact of the trawlers on the seabed habitat. To address bycatch, shrimp fishermen have voluntarily altered parts of their gear to reduce the catch of unwanted species. The commitment shown by fishermen to reduce bycatch will contribute substantially to the development of a sustainable shrimp fishery.

We believe that the seabed habitat can be conserved by establishing a network of marine protected areas. The design of a network of MPAs must leave enough room to maintain a viable commercial shrimp fleet while ensuring that portions of the seabed

1 Don't let the look of tiger shrimp at the market seduce you. Ask for prawns or shrimps that have been caught in B.C. with extruder gear. Chances are the salesperson will have no idea what you are talking about, but they will care when you walk out of the market empty handed.

2 Write a letter to the Canadian Minister of Fisheries and Oceans or the relevant government agency in your area urging the establishment of a network of marine protected areas with a core of no-take zones. (See sample letter in the Appendix.)

are set aside for conservation purposes. Conserving the seabed habitat ensures that the diverse species that live there are protected.

The establishment of MPAs will also be central to the growth of this fishery. At present, the total allowable catch per year is kept low due to lack of knowledge and poor stock assessments. Establishing no-take MPAs would allow us to study shrimp in an untouched environment, increasing our understanding of reproduction cycles and the effects of gear on habitat, eating habits, and stock levels, which in turn will lead to the growth of a sustainable fishery. Finally, marine protected areas create an insurance policy in case our regular fisheries management fails.

*J*ames Barber is best recognized as the host of the internationally acclaimed TV cooking series, *The Urban Peasant*. He is the author of eleven best-selling cookbooks, which in total have sold over a million copies. James inspired the public with his casual approach to cooking when he was chef-in-residence at Folklife during Expo 86, held in Vancouver.

Photo by John Sherlock

In addition to cooking, James has been a soldier, sailor, physicist, consulting engineer, actor, musician, writer, artist, motorcyclist, commercial fisherman, dishwasher, camp cook, and marketing salesman for the Salmon Marketing Council. He lives in Vancouver, B.C.

James Barber's Fried Shrimp and Mango Salad

¼ cup vegetable oil
1 tbsp. peppercorns
1 ½ lbs. whole shrimp, peeled
½ tsp. salt
2 tbsp. fresh ginger, grated

2 mangoes, peeled and cubed
Lettuce leaves
Spinach leaves
Juice of 1 lemon
Pepper to taste

In a medium saucepan, heat oil and add peppercorns until sizzling. Quickly sauté the shrimp for 1 to 2 minutes. Drain, dry, and toss into a mixture of salt and grated ginger. Mix with mango cubes and pile onto a plate of spinach and lettuce leaves. Just before serving, squeeze lemon juice over shrimp and sprinkle with freshly ground black pepper.

Makes 4 servings.

*C*alvin Siider, a fourth-generation fisherman, has been working in the industry almost since birth. He has been involved in many types of fishing and is currently the owner/operator of the *Maille III*, a thirty-five-foot fishing vessel with both salmon and shrimp licenses. Calvin turned to shrimping ten years ago when faced with the many crises in the salmon industry. Since then, he has demonstrated a commitment to developing a sustainable shrimp fishery.

L to R: Crystal Siider, Cailyn Siider, Scotia Siider, Kyla Sheils, JB the dog, Calvin Siider

Photo by Kelly Edwards

A concern in most fisheries is the level of bycatch. In the shrimp fishery, victims of bycatch include flatfish, pollock, and hake. Calvin says he doesn't want anything on the deck of his boat that he can't put in his hatch. Therefore he and other shrimp trawlers have developed new fishing gear which has reduced Calvin's bycatch tremendously and has proven to be very successful in most shrimping situations.

Calvin lives in Sointula, B.C. with his wife Crystal and their two daughters, Cailyn and Scotia. The whole family tries to go out fishing as often as they can. Crystal mends gillnets in one of the several net sheds around town. The following is a favourite from Crystal's collection of shrimp recipes.

Photo by Kelly Edwards

Crystal Siider's Coconut Shrimp

½ cup butter
1 large onion, chopped
2 large cloves garlic, crushed
2 tsp. ground coriander
2 tsp. turmeric
1 tsp. chili powder
½ tsp. cayenne
½ tsp. ginger
2 tbsp. white vinegar
1 cup coconut milk
1–2 lbs. large shrimp, peeled
Salt to taste
Pepper to taste
Cooked brown rice
Toasted coconut (garnish)

In a wok or skillet, heat the butter until melted, then add onions and garlic, and sauté over low heat until onions are soft. In a mortar and pestle, mix coriander, turmeric, chili powder, cayenne, and ginger with the vinegar until it becomes a paste, then add to onions. Sauté for a few minutes, stirring constantly. Add coconut milk and turn heat up to medium high. Cook until thickened. Add shrimp, season with salt and pepper, and stir until shrimp are just cooked, about 2 minutes. Serve over brown rice and sprinkle with toasted coconut.

Makes 4–6 servings.

S arah McLachlan is one of Canada's leading recording artists and a major force in the North American music industry. She has released five albums with Nettwerk Records. One of her most popular, *Surfacing*, won two Grammy Awards, four Junos, and many other distinctions. She also conceived and launched the world famous Lilith Fair, a multi-artist music festival showcasing the talent of women performers from around the world. This successful tour grossed over $28 million U.S. and donated $2 million to local and national charities. Sarah and Jaime Laurita, a chef she takes on tour to provide healthy, exciting meals for her and her band, put together *Plenty*, a book collection of their favourite recipes. The following is one of Sarah's recipes from the book.

Photo by Kharen Hill

Photo by Kelly Edwards

Sarah McLachlan's Sun-Dried Tomato and Pecan Pesto with Prawns

This pesto is also great on pasta or fish. It is easy to make in a food processor, but if you don't have one, chop the ingredients up as finely as possible. A blender is not recommended because there is not enough liquid for the blender to work properly.

2 small cloves garlic
¼ cup pecans
1–2 tbsp. olive oil
2 heaping tbsp. oil-packed sun-dried tomatoes
2 heaping tbsp. Parmesan cheese
½ cup basil leaves (spinach will do in a pinch)
1 lb. prawns, peeled and deveined
2 tbsp. butter or oil

Pesto:
In a food processor, combine garlic, pecans, olive oil, sun-dried tomatoes, cheese, and basil together and process until smooth.

In a saucepan over medium heat, sauté prawns in butter or oil until they turn pink all over, about 5–7 minutes. Toss with pesto and serve.

Makes 4 servings.

G ordie Sampson, a native of Cape Breton, Nova Scotia, is considered a major talent in the Canadian East Coast music scene. He grew up in Cape Breton and has had many accomplishments in the music industry, including the release of his album *Stones* and producing Natalie MacMaster's album *In My Hands*. Gordie's abilities as a guitarist, songwriter, and singer are undisputed. The following is one of his favourite shrimp recipes.

Gordie Sampson's Shrimp Curry

¼ **cup oil**
1 piece fresh ginger, chopped (to taste)
10 baby carrots
1 red pepper, sliced
1 cup shitake mushrooms, chopped
1 cup broccoli, chopped

½ **medium onion, chopped**
1 lb. shrimp
2 cooked chicken breasts, sliced
Juice of one lemon
2 large tomatoes, chopped
1 can curry sauce (or homemade)
Curry powder (to taste)

In a medium pot, sauté ginger, carrots, red pepper, mushrooms, broccoli, onion, shrimp, and cooked chicken in oil. Add lemon juice, cover and bring to a simmer for 15 minutes.

Add tomatoes, curry sauce, and curry powder to taste. Simmer for 10 minutes and serve over rice.

Makes 4 servings.

Wild Salmon

WILD SALMON

*I*t is virtually impossible to assess the state of salmon, given that there are five species of salmon which inhabit innumerable rivers and streams, the status of each individual river or stream can range from low to abundant. For example, in British Columbia in 2000, the Skeena River Sockeye from the North Coast are in excellent shape, while the Rivers Inlet Sockeye are in serious trouble. Fisheries managers are doing their best to protect salmon runs, and chances are any salmon on the market has come from a healthy run. If you are looking for a guilt-free salmon purchase and cannot find the type you want, try a species of salmon that *is* available.

Salmon are by far the most famous fish on the west coast. Their remarkable ability to return to the stream of their birth, where they dramatically spawn and then die, has given them worldwide recognition. How they are able to return to their streams remains one of the most fascinating mysteries of the natural world. Salmon are anadromous, meaning they grow in the ocean and spawn in the rivers. Therefore they depend on both fresh-water and marine habitat for their survival.

NO RATING: THE STATUS OF THE MANY SALMON STOCKS IN B.C. VARIES GREATLY, MAKING IT IMPOSSIBLE TO GIVE THIS FISHERY A RATING.

Although there are salmon found in other parts of the world, B.C. salmon are historically renowned for their abundance and size.

The salmon fishery employs more people than any other. Including fishermen and shareworkers, there are approximately 10,000 seasonal and full-time jobs in British Columbia in this industry. But the number of jobs and the amount of money made by salmon fishermen has declined in recent years, in part as a result of a decline in the number of salmon. This has caused severe economic hardship in coastal communities.

Loss of spawning grounds, ocean warming, disease from farmed salmon, and mismanagement of the fishery are some of the problems leading to the decline in salmon stocks. Although there are many efforts to reverse this trend, as a consumer you can help play a role in conserving salmon stocks and helping to maintain the economies of coastal communities.

One of the most interesting things about salmon is the biological uniqueness of each run. For example, the Sockeye that return to the Adams River in B.C. are genetically different from the salmon that return to the

Nimpkish River. To maintain a healthy salmon population, we need to ensure that this genetic diversity continues.

The five species of salmon caught in B.C. vary in size, colour, texture, oil content, taste, and price. Understanding the different qualities of these fish and their suitability for different types of cooking methods will make it easier for you to be flexible when purchasing salmon.

CHINOOK: Also called Spring or King salmon, it is the largest, weighing up to 100 pounds. Mostly caught by commercial trollers and much sought after by sports fishermen, its flesh colour ranges from white to deep red. The spring salmon is great for salting and pickling.

CHUM: Also called Keta or Dog salmon, the Chum has flesh that ranges from pale to medium red and is especially low in saturated fat. Chum is an excellent value for your money, and because it is one of the healthier salmon stocks, we hope that public demand will increase. These fish are nutritious, delicious, and excellent when smoked.

COHO: Most popular amongst sports fishermen, the Coho is known for its bright red colour, moderate price, and versatility. All fishing groups have been involved in efforts to conserve this type of salmon. It is hoped that

these efforts will be successful, but it is too early to tell. At present, stocks are very low and there is very little commercial fishery for it.

PINK: The Pink salmon is the smallest of the species. It is often known as the "humpy" for the hump it develops on its back at spawning time. The flesh is light-coloured and delicately flavoured. Mostly used for canned salmon, Pinks are sometimes available whole to consumers. Although this species does not keep its quality for long periods of time, it is of excellent value for your money and tastes great canned, smoked, barbecued, or baked.

1 Before shopping for salmon, contact your local fisheries office for information on the healthiest salmon runs. Request only what you think is a healthy stock at your market.

2 Try different salmon species, such as Chum or Pink, in order to take the pressure off the Sockeye fishery as well as help boost the economic opportunities of local fishermen.

SOCKEYE: The Sockeye fishery contributes two-thirds of the total value of the British Columbia salmon industry. The Sockeye's deep red flesh gives it the term "red salmon" when canned. Concerns for Sockeye stocks are increasing and conservation measures are being taken.

In British Columbia, the most talked about salmon is probably the Fraser River Sockeye. The Fraser River and its tributaries support an amazingly high number of salmon, including a large Sockeye run. When the salmon are in season, B.C. consumers look forward to purchasing fresh Sockeye for the barbecue. However, in 1998 and 1999, the stocks declined to the point where fishermen were no longer allowed to catch these fish. This decision by the Canadian Department of Fisheries and Oceans reverberated through the media, leaving the impression that salmon coast-wide where in severe difficulty.

Although the Sockeye fishery was cancelled, fishermen were still allowed to catch Chum salmon. The flesh of Chum is not as ruby red as the Sockeye, but the flavour is excellent, and especially good when used for smoking and poaching. However, low consumer demand resulted in a drop in price for Chum. In 1998, the price was so low that it was no longer economically feasible to catch the salmon, the fish plants would not buy them, and fishermen were left with no income despite availability.

Being able to purchase salmon that come from healthy runs is not easy. Every year there is a barrage of often contradictory information. One of the best ways to determine which stocks are healthy (and therefore okay to buy) is to contact the Canadian Department of Fisheries and Oceans or the relevant government agency in your area. DFO carefully monitors the streams, ensuring that enough fish return every year to spawn. Only after this has happened are fishermen allowed to catch and sell salmon. Therefore, closures, as in the case of the Fraser River Sockeye fishery, occur when there are no excess fish over the ones needed for the spawning grounds. By contacting your local fisheries office about the state of the different stocks throughout the summer, you can make informed decisions about the species you want to purchase and the area they came from.

Sockeye, Spring, and Coho salmon have traditionally been the most popular choices among consumers; however, the use of Chum and Pink salmon is growing, overcoming the initial resistance. At Living Oceans, we support this trend and urge you to get to know your salmon. The salmon season in B.C. usually starts in June with Sockeye in the northern part of the province. As the summer progresses, Sockeye runs are caught in southern areas, with the last catches of the season occurring in the Fraser River. The Chum fishery follows the Sockeye fishery, which means that Sockeye are available to consumers in early summer while Chum are available in the fall. Springs are caught throughout the summer, mostly by trollers. A lot of trollers process and freeze their fish at sea, capturing the freshness and creating a high quality product. We recommend you support your local fishermen and buy directly from them. Fresh and frozen-at-sea are the best products available.

*R*oy Henry Vickers spent the first few years of his life in the remote Tsimshian Island community of Kitkatla, between the coast of B.C. and the Queen Charlotte Islands. Several years later, the boy from Kitkatla evolved into an internationally celebrated Canadian artist whose paintings reflect his respect and caring for the planet. In Tofino, a tiny fishing village on the west coast of Vancouver Island, he has built a gallery similar to the traditional longhouse. At the Eagle Aerie Gallery, you might meet Roy and can appreciate his paintings, jewellery, books, and carvings. Today, Roy lives in Victoria where he has a studio gallery on the Tsartlip Reserve. His work is inspired by his desire to share his deep love and concern for the health of the planet with everyone he meets. We are thankful that Roy listened to the words of the famous Chief Dan George when he told him, "Roy, you have a gift. It's yours. You have to share it with people. Whatever you do, do it from your heart." This recipe comes from Roy's partner, Andrea Briggs, who has inspired him to prepare it himself. Using a hot-smoked Chum salmon that was vacuum-packed and frozen, it has been prepared and enjoyed by many people.

Photo by Kelly Edwards

Roy Henry Vickers and Andrea Briggs' Smoked Salmon Bisque

1 lb. smoked salmon, cut or broken into small pieces
³/₄ cup onions, finely chopped
2 cans tomato sauce
4 cups water
8 tbsp. butter
8 tbsp. flour
6 cups milk
3 tbsp. parsley or cilantro, finely chopped
Pepper to taste

In a large pot, combine smoked salmon, onions, tomato sauce, and water and bring to a simmer slowly for 20 minutes. Important: *do not boil*.

In a separate pot, melt butter over medium low heat and add flour. Add milk slowly, stirring constantly, followed by the parsley or cilantro. Add pepper to taste.

Add this mixture slowly to the fish mixture, being careful not to boil, and let simmer for 20 minutes.

Makes approximately 12 servings.

Ocean Master Foods of Maple Ridge, B.C. is breaking new ground by developing products that utilize Chum and Pink salmon, such as wild salmon burgers, sausages, and pizza topping. This new company is a partnership between a European sausage maker and commercial fishermen, who have combined their skills to develop new and exciting products. It is hoped that, with time, more companies will follow the ways of Ocean Master Foods and help to make the salmon market both economically and ecologically stronger. For information on their products, call Ocean Master Foods at (604) 467-8485 or email them at sales@oceanmasterfood.com.

Photo by Kelly Edwards

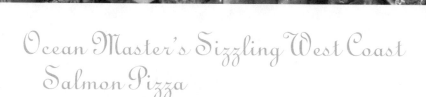

Ocean Master's Sizzling West Coast Salmon Pizza

4 oz. tomato paste
1 tbsp. whole grain mustard
¹/₃ cup cream cheese
2 red peppers, roasted and chopped
1 pizza crust
1 cup Ocean Master Pacific Salmon spicy pizza topping
1 cup mushrooms, chopped
¹/₂ cup fennel, chopped
¹/₂ red onion, chopped
¹/₂ cup mozzarella cheese
¹/₂ cup feta cheese

In a blender or food processor, mix the tomato paste, mustard, cream cheese, and roasted red pepper, and purée to a fine paste.

Spread sauce on your favourite pizza crust. Add mushrooms, fennel, and red onion and then salmon pizza topping. Add generous layer of mozzarella cheese and sprinkle with feta. Bake at 400° F for 30 minutes or until topping is well cooked.

ill Soltou has resided in Sointula, B.C., for the last twenty-seven years, during which time he has been involved in many types of fishing. He is currently owner/operator of a beautiful wooden freezer troller, the *Kaleva* (see photo), which now trolls the inside waters and

Will Soltou and his trusty deckhand: son Tucker.

Photo by Heidi Soltou

the northern B.C. coast for salmon. He and his crew take many steps to ensure a high-quality "frozen at sea" salmon; he delivers his fish to Pacific Wild Seafood, a buyer that accepts only the best in quality. For the past two years, they have awarded Will and his crew the Butterfield Quality Award, given to the fisherman who receives the highest number of quality points given at each delivery throughout the season. A large percentage of Will's fish are used for export to Europe and Japan. Here is a delicious barbecue recipe from Will and his wife Heidi.

Photo by Kelly Edwards

Will and Heidi Soltou's Barbecued Salmon with Spring Vegetables

Marinade:

½ cup sun-dried tomatoes (packed in oil), finely chopped
½ cup balsamic vinegar
4 garlic cloves, finely chopped
3 tsp. oregano
1 tsp. basil
½ cup olive oil
Juice of 1 lemon

3 tsp. walnuts, finely chopped
3 tsp. Parmesan cheese
1 tsp. pepper
Salt to taste
Splash of water (up to ¼ cup, enough to give marinade the correct consistency)

10 small new potatoes
2 salmon fillets (one whole salmon, filleted)

2 sweet red peppers, chopped
1 medium zucchini, chopped
1 white or red onion, chopped
10 cherry tomatoes
About 3 tbsp. Asiago cheese

In a blender or food processor, blend together all of the marinade ingredients. Parboil the potatoes until tender, then drain. Divide marinade in half and put half in a zip-lock bag with salmon fillets. In a bowl, toss other half of marinade with vegetables, except the cherry tomatoes. Marinate for at least 1 hour (the longer the better!).

Heat and oil the barbecue. Place marinated fish on one side of barbecue, pouring the remaining marinade on the fish. Place marinated vegetables on other side of barbecue. Cook fish until it is barely opaque. Cook vegetables, turning frequently to brown evenly. When veggies are done, toss with reserved marinade, and add cherry tomatoes and Asiago cheese. Place fish on a platter and surround with vegetables.

Makes 6–8 servings.

ynn Hunter works with the David Suzuki Foundation as their fisheries and salmon aquaculture specialist. She also works in various other capacities to address the west coast fisheries crisis, and is a member of the Board of Directors of Fisheries Renewal British Columbia, a provincial crown corporation. Her volunteer activities include membership on the Board of Directors of the Sierra Legal Defense Fund, and vice-chair of the Board of Directors of OXFAM-Canada. Lynn is also the mother of two fine adults. Her recipe, for salmon lovers, is very "hands on"—use your fingers to work the ingredients into the salmon. The result, according to Lynn, is delicious—like a candied wild salmon treat.

Lynn Hunter's Wild Soy Salmon

¾ cup soy sauce
1 cup brown sugar
2-8 oz. wild salmon filets
¼ cup whole peppercorns

In a bowl, mix the soy sauce and brown sugar and spread the mixture over the salmon filets. Take the peppercorns and, using your fingers, press them into the filets. Barbecue the filets over medium heat, covered, for about 5–7 minutes (depending on thickness of the filets). If you don't have a barbecue, you can bake the salmon in foil in a preheated 350° F oven for 20 minutes.

Makes 2 servings.

Tuna

TUNA

In recent years, tuna has been reinvented, elevated from ordinary sandwich filler to extraordinary gourmet dinner. The meaty flesh of fresh tuna, seared rare, is perfect for barbecues and grilling. As more and more people begin enjoying new ways of cooking it, tuna is finding its way on to the tables of many a connoisseur.

There are at least seventy-five species of tuna, ranging in length from a couple of inches to the giant Blue Fin tuna, which reaches some thirteen feet in length. Tuna are a warm-blooded fish and do not have a swim bladder; therefore, they must remain constantly on the move to avoid sinking. Tuna travel great distances, sometimes crossing entire oceans in short amounts of time. It is thought that on their long seasonal journeys they follow ocean currents using the sun as a compass to navigate. These fish are built for speed with their narrow-forked, crescent-shaped tails and muscle-bound bodies. As adults, their speed is one of their greatest defences. By studying the design of tuna, engineers have improved the performance of submarines.

Tuna are seldom seen near coasts, preferring to swim in offshore areas where their food is abundant.

CURRENTLY THE STATUS OF STOCKS IS UNKNOWN, BUT BELIEVED TO BE HEALTHY.

Spawning also takes place offshore, a process which involves broadcasting spawn into the ocean. Large amounts of eggs are released but only a portion reach maturity; many eggs and juvenile fish become food for other ocean creatures.

Young tuna grow quickly and remain near the surface for the first two years of their life. Groups of young tuna usually stick together in schools as a form of defence against predators. They feed largely on shrimp-sized creatures abundant in the ocean. Their main enemies are seals, orcas, and sea lions, but as young fish they are vulnerable to all sorts of ocean predators.

Like many other species of seafood, shopping for sustainably caught tuna means knowing a bit about the different species available. Yellow Fin tuna are commonly purchased as canned tuna. They are the ones that swim with dolphins and at one time were be caught using large drift nets, but public outrage about the bycatch of dolphins led to the elimination of ninety-seven percent of the world's drift nets. Yellow Fin tuna are also caught with seine gear. Fishermen can avoid or reduce the number of dolphins they catch if they take the necessary precautions. Some cans of tuna are marked "dolphin safe," meaning they are caught with gear that does not harm the dolphins; however, there are concerns that this labelling is not accurate. The only truly dolphin-safe tuna is albacore. So when purchasing canned tuna, look for albacore on the label.

Another well-known species of tuna is the Blue Fin. These large, mighty creatures live off the east coast of the United States and have been a favourite among recreational fishermen for years. The commercial fleet has also targeted this fishery to the point where the stocks have now seriously declined. Consumers should avoid buying blue fin tuna at all times.

The only species that is caught by B.C. fishermen is the Albacore. These relatively small tuna, measuring about 2.5 feet long, migrate great distances; one tuna was tagged off the coast of California and then recaptured off the coast of Japan a year later, a distance of nearly 5,000 miles. As a result of their long migration route, it is often difficult to assess the state of the stocks; however, scientists in both Canada and the United States believe the albacore tuna fishery, which is international and managed through a Canada/U.S. agreement, is healthy. Albacore tuna do not travel with dolphins, so bycatch is not an issue. In fact, fishermen in B.C. use trolling gear, which targets only tuna, making it one of the cleanest fisheries in B.C.

Increasingly, consumers are recognizing tuna as a high quality product. It is rich in Omega 3 oils which have been associated with lowering the risk of heart disease and breast cancer, among other maladies, and may also help ease the symptoms of such ailments as manic depression, making tuna good to eat and good for you. There is so much more to tuna than making sandwiches and once you've tried other ways of eating it, you will be hooked.

As with much seafood, firmness is important when checking tuna for quality. High quality albacore that has been bled and frozen properly is very firm, whereas poor quality tuna is very mushy.

CONSERVATION TIPS

1 Always purchase albacore tuna, either fresh or canned.

2 If your local market does not carry albacore tuna, ask the manager to start ordering it.

3 Look for our yearly updates about which fish are okay to purchase. We will let you know if the stocks are declining and if further action needs to be taken.

When Patti Sloan fell in love with salmon fisherman Chris Sloan in the spring of 1986, little did she realize how much her life would change. In order to be with him as much as possible, she joined him at sea for the fishing season. Before long she fell in love not only with a fisherman but the fishing way of life as well. In 1988, their daughter Maquinna went on her first fishing trip at the age of three weeks. Daughter Nicola joined the clan in 1990 and they have been a fishing family ever since. Patti says fishing together has made them very close as a

Nicola and Maquinna Sloan in fish scale

Photo by Patti Sloan

family, especially living in such small quarters. The girls have learned to be creative about entertaining themselves as well as becoming good friends, as there are no other children to play with while at sea.

When the salmon fishery went through some drastic changes in the 1990s, the Sloan family was also forced to make changes; in 1997, they bought the Sea Hunter, a larger vessel with a freezer on board. This made it possible for the family to fish for tuna in offshore waters. Since then tuna fishing has become an important part of their lives. Following are two of Patti's favourite ways to prepare tuna.

Patti Sloan's Tuna Melt

1 can Albacore tuna (or leftover cooked tuna)
1 cup mayonnaise (to moisten)
1 medium onion, chopped
2 stalks celery, chopped
1 tsp. lemon juice
1 tsp. parsley
1 tsp. dill weed
Salt to taste
Pepper to taste
4 English muffins
1 cup cheddar cheese, grated

Mix together well the tuna, mayonnaise, onion, celery, lemon juice, parsley, dill weed, and salt and pepper. Toast the English muffins and place on a baking sheet. Cover muffins with tuna mixture and top with grated cheese. Place in a heated oven until cheese melts and is very lightly browned. Serve with a knife and fork.

Makes 4 servings.

The Sloan Family's Not-So-Secret Teriyaki Tuna

4–5 cloves garlic, minced
1 piece fresh ginger, minced
$^1/_2$ cup light soy sauce
2 tbsp. sake

$^1/_2$ tsp. sugar
4 Albacore tuna steaks
Sesame seeds (garnish; optional)

Sauce:

In a food processor, place garlic cloves and fresh ginger and process until minced. Add soy sauce, sake, and sugar, and process again until mixed well. Place in a covered jar until ready for use (this can be done up to a week in advance). If you don't have a food processor, mince garlic and ginger with a knife, then mix with the soy sauce, sake, and sugar.

If you are using a whole tuna, it is easiest to prepare it when it is partially frozen. Cut the tuna into steaks using a very sharp knife. Trim skin and dark meat if desired. The darker meat is stronger tasting and is considered waste to some and a delicacy to others. Steaks can be left as such or cut into cubes for shish kabobs. Both work well for this recipe.

Marinate tuna steaks or cubes in the prepared sauce for an hour. If making kabobs, thread tuna and any good grilling vegetables of your choice, on pre-soaked bamboo skewers.

Heat barbecue until it is very hot, making sure the rails are clean and well-oiled. Grill the tuna steaks until they are lined with dark grill marks, then flip them over to grill the other sides.

Timing depends on the thickness of the tuna and how hot the grill is. If the fish is approximately $1^1/_2$ inches thick, grill for 5 minutes per side and then check a piece to see if it is done to your liking. Make sure you don't overcook it! Tuna is best prepared on the rare side.

Top steaks with sesame seeds just before taking them off the grill. This recipe also works well on a stove-top grill or under the broiler. Makes 4 servings.

as mentioned in the chapter on halibut, Natalie MacMaster is an internationally known fiddler. Here is her recipe for Tuna Broccoli Quiche:

Natalie MacMaster's Crustless Tuna Broccoli Quiche

1 tbsp. butter
1 medium onion, chopped
1 cup broccoli, chopped
1 cup milk
4 eggs
³⁄₄ cup Bisquick baking mix
¹⁄₂ tsp. salt
¹⁄₄ tsp. pepper
7 oz. canned tuna
1 cup shredded Swiss cheese

In a skillet, heat butter. Add onion and sauté for 4 minutes until translucent. Add broccoli and sauté for 1 minute longer. In a bowl, beat together milk, eggs, baking mix, salt, and pepper. Fold in canned tuna, cheese, and onion-broccoli mixture. Pour into greased 10-inch pie plate. Cover with grated cheese. Bake at 400° F for 30 to 40 minutes. Let stand for five minutes.

Crabs

CRABS

*D*ungeness crabs are known all over the world for their superior quality, texture, and unbeatable taste. They are an excellent source of high-quality protein, contain all essential amino acids, and offer a rich supply of important minerals such as zinc, copper, calcium, magnesium, and iron. Crabs are low in fat and calories and are a natural choice for health-conscious consumers. And according to the Canadian Department of Fisheries and Oceans, they are an ideal species for managing and fishing. Most importantly, crabs are fun to eat!

Like all fisheries, the key to building a sustainable fishery for crabs is ensuring that every year there are enough crabs left to reproduce, thereby providing the next generation. To reach this goal in Canada, the DFO has placed limits on the size of crabs that can be caught: they must be 6.5 inches wide at the broadest part of the shell or carapace. This size ensures that sexually mature male crabs have had at least one year to reproduce before being caught. Females rarely reach this size and therefore are able to reproduce every year. We believe that all female crabs, even those exceeding 6.5 inches, should be set free to ensure the successful regeneration of the stocks.

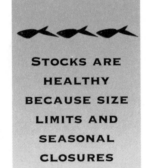

STOCKS ARE HEALTHY BECAUSE SIZE LIMITS AND SEASONAL CLOSURES CONTRIBUTE TO A WELL-MANAGED FISHERY.

Dungeness crabs are found all along the west coast, from the Aleutian Islands in Alaska to the waters off California. It is said that the name Dungeness comes from the old town of the same name, where they were harvested commercially in the mid-1800s. Dungeness crabs are not picky eaters: they eat almost anything, including clams, starfish, sea worms, squid, snails, and even other crabs. And as far as crabs being targets themselves: humans are not the only ones that consume them; large fish, eels, and octopus also eat them.

Crabs grow by shedding their old shells in a process known as molting. During the first couple years of life, crabs molt several times. The process takes only about fifteen minutes, but the crab remains vulnerable to predators for at least forty-eight hours before its new shell hardens. Some crabs consume their own recently molted shells in order to quickly supply their bodies with the nutrients needed to harden their new shells. The next time you see what looks like a dead crab on the beach, look closely and you might find it is the discarded shell that a crab outgrew.

Crabs have the amazing ability to regenerate new legs or pinchers if they happen to lose one, most often as they are trying to escape a predator. The crab is able to release the injured appendage with a minimum of bleeding, and a stub is rapidly formed where the limb once was. Then, over a series of molts, it grows a new, functioning limb.

The commercial crab season varies throughout the coast and is based on the crabs' molting season. The limits placed on the length of the crab-fishing season by fisheries managers is meant to cause as little harm as possible to both molting and undersized crabs. Handling of crabs during fisheries can result in injury, especially in the molting season when the shells are very soft. Fishermen are expected to return both soft-shell and undersized crabs back to the ocean. Doing this consistently and with tender loving care will help to ensure the continued health of the crab fishery.

The illegal harvesting of undersized specimens is an ongoing problem that poses a serious threat not only to the Dungeness crab, but to the livelihoods of crab fishermen as well. If this problem continues, fisheries managers may impose early closures in specific areas. If you suspect illegal crab harvesting, it is important to notify your local fisheries office. The future of the fishery and the crab stocks depends on it.

Dungeness crab landings all along the west coast are above historic levels as markets continue to grow and develop. Currently, there are 222 commercial crab licences in B.C. Licence stacking is not permitted in this fishery, meaning that for every license there is a job for at least one person.

Crabs are caught in circular steel traps commonly called "pots," which weigh between sixty and 125 pounds, with a diameter of thirty-six to forty-eight inches. These pots are marked with buoys attached to a length of rope so that they can be easily retrieved. They can be baited with herring, squid, ground fish, or razor clams.

Fishermen deliver live male Dungeness crabs to processing plants where they are either prepared to be air-freighted live for the fresh market, or cooked and packed for the processed market. Dungeness crabs are

1 If you're shopping for crabs, make sure you're buying ones of legal size. If you're setting a crab trap to catch your own (if legal), make sure you only take males and, again, that they are of legal size. If your trap catches any other critters or undersized crabs, carefully release them back into the ocean.

twenty to twenty-five percent meat by weight. The succulent white meat from the legs and the body is highly prized for crab cocktails, pastas, pastries, sauces, and salads. But many prefer the simple, sublime method of an old-fashioned crab boil, scooping out the meat and eating it directly from the shell.

inger Mary Jane Lamond earned East Coast Music Association nominations for Female Artist, Album, and Entertainer for her latest CD, *Làn Dùil*, which was also nominated for a Juno Award as Best Roots/Traditional Solo Album. Mary Jane first fell in love with Scottish Gaelic traditions and song while in Nova Scotia visiting her grandparents throughout her youth. Despite the important role her music plays in preserving Scottish Gaelic musical traditions that would otherwise rarely be heard outside Cape Breton, Mary Jane Lamond says her primary purpose is to entertain. Here is Mary Jane's recipe for an East Coast favourite.

Mary Jane Lamond's East Coast Crab Cakes

14 oz. crab meat, cooked
¹/₂ cup red pepper, finely chopped
1 cup green onion, finely chopped
2 eggs, beaten
4 tbsp. lemon juice
4 tsp. Dijon mustard
1 pinch black pepper
2 ¹/₂ cups dried bread crumbs
¹/₄ cup vegetable oil

In a large bowl, mix crab meat, red pepper, green onion, eggs, lemon juice, mustard, and pepper with 2 to 3 tablespoons of bread crumbs. Form mixture into patties and roll in remaining breadcrumbs. In a non-stick pan, fry the cakes in oil until lightly browned, turning once.

Makes 4 servings.

Photo by Kelly Edwards

F ishing is a way of life for eight-year-old Conner Siider and his family. At the age of six months, Conner was lounging in a swing from the mast of his parents' fishing boat while they trolled for sockeye salmon. Conner is now turning out to be an excellent deckhand, working alongside his dad. Conner says he hopes to be a fifth-generation fisherman when he grows up; the truth, although he doesn't realize it yet, is that he already is.

Living in a small fishing community, seafood is inherently an important part of Conner's diet. His two favourite meals are shrimp from his uncle Calvin (see the shrimp chapter) and crab. The following is Conner's personal steps for catching and eating crab.

A Crab Feast at the Siider House

1. If you are cleaning fish, save all your scraps and place them in the freezer in an old plastic container. When you are ready to set your crab trap, take out the container and use the scraps for bait. If you do not have any fish scraps, use any meat that has a strong smell.

2. Take your trap, a rope, and container full of bait down to the wharf. (Don't forget to wear your lifejacket.) Poke holes in the bottom of the plastic container containing the scraps and place it in the trap.

3. Close up the trap, tie the rope to it, and lower it into the water, holding the rope tight. When the trap has touched the bottom, tie the end of the rope to the dock.

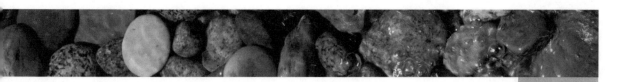

4. Wait until the next day before you check your trap.

5. Before going to check the trap, take a large, deep pot and fill it three-quarters full with water, adding enough salt to flavour it. Place the pot on the stove, cover with a lid, and turn heat to medium high. Leave an adult at home to watch the water. (Moms do a good job with this.)

6. Take a large bucket and a ruler with you when you go to check your trap. Pull up your trap and look at the crabs you've caught to see if they are male or female. The best way to tell the difference is to look at their undersides: those that have V-shaped markings are males, and those that have U-shaped markings are females. (The crabs with V bellies you can keep and the crabs with U bellies go back in the water to have babies and make more crabs.) Measure the male crabs with your ruler; keep only the ones that are 6.5 inches or more.

7. Bring your male crabs home and put them straight into your pot of boiling water (don't let them pinch you) for fifteen minutes. When ready, pour into the sink and rinse.

8. When the cooked crabs are cool enough to handle, break them in half, remove their guts, then rinse and place in the fridge to cool further.

9. Return the pot to the stove. Peel and chop 3 cloves of garlic and place in the pot with ½ cup of butter. Heat until the butter is melted.

10. Now for the best part: Spread out a used newspaper on the table, crack open the crab, dip in the melted garlic butter, then eat. When finished with your meal, roll up the shells in the newspaper and bury in your mom's garden; it makes great fertilizer for her flowers and vegetables.

Kim West was born in Vancouver, B.C. She graduated from the University of British Columbia in 1978, having started working for the Canadian Department of Fisheries and Oceans as a student in her third year. Kim has worked for the department for twenty-two years in various capacities, including Design and Feasibility and Assessment Biologist with the Salmon Enhancement Program, Habitat Biologist, and presently as the Management Biologist for Shellfish and Minor Finfish with the Fraser River Division. She is married with two delightful children, Douglas and Kelsey. She lives with her family in Vancouver and enjoys spending time in the summer sailing up and down the west coast of B.C. The following is Kim's version of a Japanese favourite; the nori and wasabi are available in Asian markets.

Kim West's California Roll

1 cup sushi rice
1 ¼ cup water
2 tbsp. rice vinegar
½ tsp. sugar
1tsp. salt
1 package of *nori* (seaweed sheet)
Japanese mayonnaise
Prepared *wasabi* (Japanese horseradish)
1 avocado, peeled and thinly sliced
1 small cucumber, julienned
½ cup cooked crab meat
5 stalks green onion, cut into 6-inch lengths

In a medium pot, prepare sushi rice as you would any other rice by boiling in water. In a separate pot, heat the rice vinegar, sugar, and salt, then add to the rice after it is cooked and still warm.

Take 1 sheet of sushi *nori* and cover with a layer of the sushi rice mixture. Add a thin line of Japanese mayonnaise and a small amount of the prepared *wasabi* along bottom edge of rice. (Remember that *wasabi* is very hot and spicy so be careful how much you add; this can be omitted.)

On top of the mayonnaise and *wasabi*, lay avocado, cucumber, crab meat, and green onions and roll from the bottom edge (where all the goodies are) to the top edge.

Cut crosswise into 8 bite-sized medallions. Serve with soya sauce and additional wasabi (for dipping).

Makes 1 roll.

Photo by Simon Desrochers

*E*legant yet cozy, the Sooke Harbour House on B.C.'s Vancouver Island was rated the best restaurant in Canada by *The Globe and Mail* and the second-best country inn in the world in the May 2000 edition of *Gourmet* magazine. The restaurant at the Sooke Harbour House specializes in west coast Canadian cuisine, especially seafood, and much of its produce comes from the inn's gardens or nearby farms. The Sooke Harbour House specializes in seasonal, local, and organic foods and is strongly supportive of organic products. It composts its waste materials, recycles its water, and does not use genetically modified organisms or farmed fish in its kitchen. In fact, it has actively participated in public campaigns against the use of farmed salmon. In practice, the Sooke Harbour House strongly supports the concepts of sustainable agriculture and a sustainable fishery and, consequently, we support the Sooke Harbour House. The following recipe is from chef Peter Zambri.

Photo by Kelly Edwards

Sooke Harbour House's Crab Consommé

1 Spanish onion, chopped
1 carrot, chopped
1 celery stalk, chopped
1 leek, chopped
1 medium red pepper, chopped
2 bay leaves
1 ½ lb. Red Rock or Dungeness
   crab meat, cooked (plus shells)
2 egg whites
8 oz. dry vermouth

4 cups strong clear fish stock
4 cups strong clear chicken stock
1 tbsp. tomato paste
2 cups mixed savoury garden herbs
   (e.g., flat-leaf parsley, tarragon,
   rosemary, lemon thyme, chives)
2 juniper berries
Low-sodium *tamari* to taste
   (optional; available in Asian
   markets)

In a food processor, coarsely chop onion, carrot, celery, leek, red pepper, and bay leaves. Add the crab meat by hand and stir, then add the crab shells and egg whites.

In a large pot, pour in vermouth, then fish and chicken stocks. Stir in crab-egg white-vegetable mixture, then add tomato paste, herbs, and juniper berries. Place pot over medium heat and carefully stir occasionally to ensure nothing sticks to the bottom. When a raft (coagulated vegetable and crab mixture) starts to form, the agitation process will cease. Be patient; this process will take about 15 minutes. Turn heat down to a slow simmer.

The consommé should simmer for approximately 1 hour before raft is fully formed. Be sure not to boil rapidly or raft will separate and a complete mess will follow. The raft will feel firm to the touch, not smooth and mushy.

Remove from the pot with a large ladle and strain consommé through cheesecloth and strainer into another pot. Adjust for seasoning with tamari if desired and serve at once, or cool, chill, and reheat when desired.

Makes 4 servings.

*D*r. Elliott Norse, president and founder of the Marine Conservation Biology Institute (MCBI), played an important role in the development of the concept of biological diversity. After receiving his Ph.D. in Marine Ecology, during which time he studied crabs in the Caribbean, Elliott held various positions, including Staff Ecologist of the President's Council on Environmental Quality, Public Policy Director of the Ecological Society of America, and Chief Scientist for the Center for Marine Conservation. In 1996, he founded MCBI, where he brought together prominent scientists to address issues that threaten the conservation of marine biological diversity. To date, he has done extensive work on introduced species, global warming, and bottom trawling. He recently played a key role in President Clinton's commitment to establish a network of MPAs in American waters. One of Elliott's special talents is his ability to explain the complexity of our oceans to people of all ages with humour, warmth, and a sense of wonder. Elliott lives in Redmond, Washington with his wife Irene. According to his staff, Elliott is a wonderful cook, and this tasty crab recipe is proof of that.

Photo by Kelly Edwards

Elliott Norse's Dungeness Crab Delight

Water
4 large live Dungeness crabs (1 per person)
¼ cup canola oil
¼ lb. fresh ginger, unpeeled, sliced large
20 medium stalks green onions
¼ cup soy sauce

In a large pot, pour 1 ½ inches of water, and bring to a furious boil. Place the crabs in and cover with a tight-fitting lid. If pot is not large enough, steam one or two at a time. Steam them for 12–15 minutes to a merciful death.

Remove crabs from pot and rinse with cold water until they are cool enough to handle. Remove carapace from top of each crab by holding back legs in one hand and lifting carapace off from back to front. Then remove gills and soft matter. What you are left with is body meat and legs, all attached. Chop or break crabs in half.

In a large, deep 14-inch wok or frying pan, heat canola oil, and add large slices of ginger. Fry ginger until it starts to brown, then add crabs, 2 at a time if possible, turning several times. After 2 minutes, add the base of the scallions (the white part, minus roots in 2-inch lengths). Cook crabs for an additional 2 minutes on the other side, then add the green parts of the green onions and soy sauce. Crabs are wonderful with a white wine like Gewurtz Traminer or a light red wine.

Makes 4 servings.

$\mathcal{K}$aren Barnaby loves fish. She has been overseeing the kitchen operations at The Fish House in Stanley Park in Vancouver since 1995, and is the author of the cookbooks *Pacific Passions* and *Screamingly Good Food*, and co-author of *The Girls Who Dish* series. Karen teaches on a regular basis, sharing her love for simple cooking with enthusiastic audiences. She is an active volunteer as the president of Les Dames d'Escoffier, an organization that raises scholarships for women in or wishing to enter the food service industry. While there are still requests for seafood on the "no-no" list, The Fish House in Stanley Park has made the commitment to serving sustainable seafood while balancing the needs of the business. Karen says, "Dungeness crab was another glorious reward for moving west. While I enjoy it chilled with a lemony mayonnaise, this recipe is for those of you who, like me, feel that digging into a drippy, savory crab transcends all other eating experiences."

Photo by Kelly Edwards

Karen Barnaby's Herb and Parmesan Roasted Dungeness Crab

2 2-lb. Dungeness crabs, cooked
1 ¹/₂ tsp. fennel seeds, coarsely crushed
¹/₂ cup parsley, coarsely chopped
¹/₂ cup fresh basil leaves, coarsely chopped
4 cloves garlic, minced
¹/₄ tsp. cayenne pepper
2 tsp. paprika
¹/₂ tsp. salt
1 tsp. black pepper, freshly ground
¹/₃ cup extra-virgin olive oil
¹/₂ cup Parmesan cheese, freshly grated

After crabs have been boiled, remove top shells and gills and the soft matter in the middle. Cut crabs in half and crack the legs.

Combine fennel seeds, parsley, basil, garlic, cayenne, paprika, salt, pepper, and olive oil. Place crabs in a shallow baking dish that holds them comfortably in a single layer. Pour herb mixture over crabs and toss to coat them well. Cover and refrigerate for 2 hours.

Preheat oven to 400° F. Sprinkle crab with Parmesan cheese and roast on top rack of oven until golden brown, about 10 minutes. Serve immediately.

Makes 4 appetizer servings or 2 main course servings.

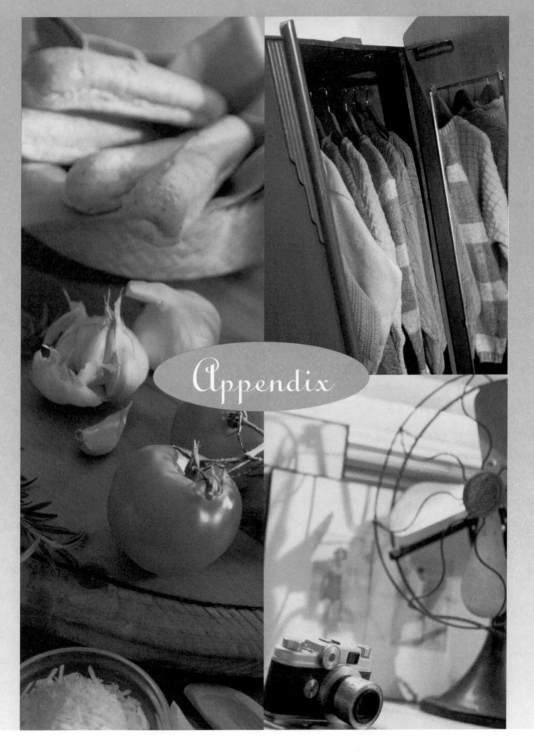

Appendix

FISHING METHODS

These are the principal methods of commercial fishing in British Columbia. Fisheries in other areas may use other techniques in addition to these.

DIVING: Some species, such as octopus, geoduck, sea urchins, and sea cucumber, are taken commercially in the dive fisheries. These species are handpicked and brought to the surface where they are placed in boats. At the end of the day, they are taken in for processing.

GILLNETTING: Gillnetters use regulated sized nets that attach to drums on small boats, and are strung close to the shore. The fishermen continually tend their nets when they are in the water. Gillnetters fish mainly for Sockeye and Chum near coastal rivers and inlets. The way in which the nets are suspended in the water, and the choice of net sizes, allows them to target specific species. New regulations have limited sets to a specific amount of time to increase the odds of survival of bycatch.

HAND-LINING: Hand-lining or jigging is one of the oldest forms of fishing. It is simply a hooked line going from the boat into the water held down with a weight and pulled up by hand or with pulleys.

Fishermen have different techniques for hand-lining. This method is used for the live rockfish and lingcod fisheries.

LONG-LINING: Long-lining is exactly what its name implies: a long line that is set out with baited hooks attached. A rope or line is rolled off a drum, bated hooks are attached, and the rope slowly sinks to the bottom. A buoy or marker is attached at either end and floats at the surface so fishermen can keep track of their gear. These strings are left for a certain amount of time and then hauled back onto the boat. Hooks are removed from the rope, fish are taken off, and the rope winds back on to the drum. When the whole string has been picked up, the process is repeated. This method is used for halibut, black cod, and some rockfish.

PURSE SEINING: This is one of the most efficient ways to catch large volumes of salmon close to the surface. Seining involves encircling the fish with a net up to a quarter-mile long. Pulling the purse line, much like a drawstring purse, closes the bottom of the net. The fish now cannot escape and the net is slowly pulled aboard the boat. As the net is pulled aboard, the purse line enclosing the fish becomes smaller and smaller. When the circle is very tight and the fish are very concentrated, the fish are pulled aboard or are scooped out with a dipnet in a process called brailing.

The variations in seine fishing arise from different methods of pulling the net. It can be wound onto a drum, or run through a power block on the boom and piled on to the stern. In the salmon fishery, seines catch mainly Sockeyes, Pinks, and Chums. Seine boats now use scoop nets to remove fish from encircled nets, which allows them to be selective in their catch.

TRAPS: Traps are weighted, baited, and set out one at a time, or attached to a rope and set out in a series. Traps sink to the bottom and are marked with buoys. They are left for a designated amount of time depending on many different factors, such as weather conditions, targeted species, or preferences of the fishermen. Traps are used for prawns, crabs, and sablefish.

TRAWLING: There are two main types of trawling on the west coast: otter and beam. They all use similar nets, but the size of the gear changes for each fishery. Cone-shaped nets are towed with steel cables at relatively slow speeds. After a towing period of several hours, the net is hauled on board, the catch is

released on to the deck, sorted, processed, and stored until delivery. For conservation purposes, net sizes that allow the escape of small fish are mandatory.

Otter trawling is given its name for the rectangle-shaped doors or otterboards. The purpose of these doors is to work with the movement of the boat to keep the cone open. Otter trawl gear is used for both bottom trawling and mid-water trawling. When bottom trawling for groundfish such as ocean perch or lingcod, weights are attached to the bottom and floats are attached to the top. The net rolls along close to the bottom with the aid of wheel-like bobbins. Otter trawl gear is mostly used by bigger boats in the shrimp and groundfish fishery. In mid-water trawling, fewer weights are used to adjust towing depths throughout the water. In Canada, huge boats fish hake using this method.

Beam trawling is a historical fishing method that was originally developed by the Japanese. It dates back to the days of sail-powered fishing vessels, and gets its name from the beam used to keep the cone-shaped nets open. The metal or wooden beam is attached between each side of the net and keeps it open while the fishing vessel tows it along the bottom. This method is used mostly by the smaller boats in the west coast shrimp fishery.

TROLLING: Trollers handle their fish one at a time and concentrate on the higher quality species of salmon. Trollers are generally smaller vessels, with smaller crews. The vessels move slowly along towing lines with hooks on the end. The fish are pulled on board one at a time and then bled and cleaned (or dressed). After being washed clean of blood, the fish are then put in the hatch for storage. Trollers can store their fish using three different methods: iceboats store their fish in layers of ice, slush boats store their fish in a mixture of water and ice, and most freezer boats freeze their fish on trays and glaze them in saltwater, stacking them in their hatch. Ice trollers can stay out at sea for up to ten days while freezer trollers only need to come in for supplies. Trolling methods are use for salmon, albacore, and lingcod.

Glossary of Terms

BROADCAST SPAWN: A reproductive process in which both the male and female expel their reproductive cells into the water.

BROUGHTON ARCHIPELAGO: A group of islands located between northern Vancouver Island and the Mainland with many communities dependent on its abundantly rich marine life.

BYCATCH: The unintended catch of certain species. This occurs because different species share habitat; for example, Yellow Fin tuna travel with dolphins and rockfish cohabitate with halibut. Unwanted bycatch is often thrown back into the water; however, some species, particularly rockfish, will not survive. When thrown back into the water, the species may serve as food for other sea life, but it does not contribute to the reproduction cycle. Fishermen and scientists continue working towards solutions to bycatch problems. We have come a long way since the days of killing everything that is not of direct use to us. Extruder devices in shrimp trawls minimize bycatch. While short gillnet sets and using a scooped net when seining, a process called brailing allows the live release of unwanted species. These examples show us we are on the road to creating clean, healthy fisheries.

COMMERCIAL FISHING: The act of fishing for the purpose of selling your catch.

EDMUNDS UNDERWATER PRESERVE: A two-kilometre area in Puget Sound, Washington that has been closed to fishing for twenty-seven years.

FISHERIES: The commercial fishing industry is divided into different fisheries. This divisions are done according to species, gear type, and area.

FLATFISH: Any number of a species of thin, flat fish that swim on one side with both eyes located on the side that faces up while swimming. Size and colour vary depending on the species. Flatfish usually have lean, translucent flesh that is very tasty. Common flatfish include halibut, sole, flounder, and turbot.

INDIVIDUAL VESSEL QUOTA: Amount of catch allocated to a vessel.

INVERTEBRATE: Animal without a backbone—about 95 percent of all animals on Earth. Includes everything from one-celled organisms such as amoebas to sponges, corals, anemones, worms, crustaceans, molluscs, and enchinoderms.

LEGAL HARVESTABLE SIZE LIMIT: A designated size that allows for the reproduction of a species.

MARINE PROTECTED AREAS: At Living Oceans Society, we believe that the only way to protect vital spawning, rearing, and nursery areas is to implement MPAs that contain the following elements:

Core no-take areas that prohibit commercial and recreational fishing, exploration for and extraction of oil, gas, and minerals, open net cage aquaculture, bottom trawling, dumping, and dredging.

Buffer zones that permit fishing but prohibit activities that disrupt the seabed habitat, such as exploration and extraction of oil, gas, and minerals, open net cage aquaculture, bottom trawling, dumping, and dredging.

Additional activities such as sewage outfalls, log booming and dumping, recreational artificial reefs, could be prohibited on a case-by-case basis.

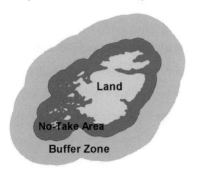

OPTIMAL LEVELS: When a species has reached a maximum level of population.

STOCK STATUS REPORT: A report assembled by biologists estimating the population of a specific species.

SUBTIDAL ENVIRONMENT: The habitat in the part of the ocean just below the low tide line.

SUSTAINABLE FISHERIES: Catching fish at a rate that doesn't result in the decline of the optimum population. This will ensure we are meeting the needs of today without compromising the needs of future generations.

SWIM BLADDER: A thin, walled sac in some fish that functions as a buoyancy control device, allowing the fish to adjust to different depths.

TOTAL ALLOWABLE CATCH: A catch limit placed on fisheries for the purpose of maintaining healthy stocks.

SAMPLE LETTER

This letter is specific to Canadian government agencies and practices, but it is also applicable to other countries in which fisheries are threatened.

The Honourable (Name of Minister of Fisheries and Oceans)

Minister of Fisheries and Oceans

House of Commons

Ottawa, Ontario

KIA-OA6

Date

Dear

Fish stocks are collapsing all over the world. (THE FOLLOWING IS SPECIFIC TO CONCERNS IN BRITISH COLUMBIA; COMMENTS SPECIFIC TO YOUR AREA CAN BE INSERTED HERE.) More specifically, in British Columbia, the abalone fishery has been closed due to overfishing, rockfish stocks are declining, and lingcod harvesting is closed in the Strait of Georgia. We need to find ways to prevent further disasters and rebuild our depleted stocks for the sake of the environment and the people who depend on them.

I believe that setting up a network of marine protected areas with a core of no-take zones is a step towards maintaining healthy stocks and healthy fisheries. By rebuilding healthy stocks we will be creating fisheries that will last for years to come. Creating sustainable fisheries is a challenge that needs your attention and support. I urge you to consider establishing a network of marine protected areas with a core of no-take zones to ensure our fisheries for future generations.

Sincerely,

A U T H O R N O T E S

*L*ike many projects, this cookbook started as a pipedream. I had just started Living Oceans Society when I thought a project like this would be a new and innovative way to increase awareness about our ocean and our fisheries. With all the work that comes with launching a new conservation organization, I tucked this idea on a back shelf, hoping one day to dust it off.

A few short months later, Karen Sommer approached me about working for Living Oceans Society through a retraining program. Formally a fisherman, Karen was looking for a new career that allowed her to stay at home with her two young children. I offered her the challenge of writing this book and she took it eagerly.

It has been a challenging experience for both of us. I came to this project strictly from the position of an environmentalist. Karen, on the other hand, brought incredible insight into the fishing community. Reconciling these two views has made us wrestle with some issues and often made us reflect on our personal views on conservation and commercial fisheries. Karen taught me a great deal about the commitment of fishermen to make B.C.'s fisheries sustainable, and without her involvement this book would not be as comprehensive as it is. I am forever indebted to her for her insight.

As the publisher's deadline loomed near, we recruited Oonagh O'Connor to give us a hand. Oonagh jumped in with both feet and quickly became immersed in the researching and writing for this book. Without her help, Karen and I may have gotten lost in the netherworld of recipes and stock status reports.

Other people to thank are numerous and I could never list them all. In particular I would like to thank my mother Jane for instilling the love of cooking in me, and my father John for sharing with me the joy of fishing for bass early in the morning at the cottage. The many hours that I work are made easy with the unconditional support and home cooking from my husband Bruce, and I am forever indebted to him. Thanks to our dog Lucy for making me leave the office for walks on the beach, keeping me close to the source of my inspiration. Finally, thanks to my many friends from Halifax to B.C., who make me laugh when I get too serious and make my life richer.

When I first thought of this project I never thought it would really come to fruition. Happily, I have been proven wrong. This experience has reminded me that, with the determined commitment of co-workers and the support of friends and family, even pipedreams can come true. I will keep this lesson close to heart as we move forward in our efforts to conserve our marine environment and the communities that depend on it.

—Jennifer Lash

*H*elping Jen and Karen with this book has been such an educational experience. Learning about the incredible natures of some of the ocean's creatures has increased my respect for the sea. Realizing how dedicated some fishermen are in developing sustainable fishing techniques has also been a real eye-opener. We don't hear enough about how hard fishermen work to ensure that fishing will continue to be an option for their grandchildren. Living in this community and working on this book has made me realize that fishing is not just a job, it's a way of life.

I think one of the most important messages of this book is how much power we have as consumers. We can make a difference! What we buy and don't buy can determine the market and the future survival of coastal communities. As I worked on this book I began to envision a world where we refuse to support restaurants that serve farmed salmon; where stores are forced to sell only wild salmon because we, the consumers, won't settle for anything less. I hope this book contributes to making this vision a reality.

Thanks to all the fishermen and other people who continue to

work hard to develop sustainable fishing. And thanks
to my son Sean for being so patient waiting for his
mom while she edits one more sentence. And of
course, thanks to my partner Eddie who taught me
how to harvest my first fish with respect.

—Oonagh O'Connor

This book is about using and appreciating the bounty of the sea while understanding that we are all part of the bigger picture. We need to live and fish gently within the capacities of our living home, Earth. Building sustainable fisheries means creating fisheries for our future without sacrificing the fisheries of today; it means the continued survival of a lifestyle that is precious and vital to our fishing communities. To develop sustainable fisheries, we must acquire the knowledge we need to avoid repeating mistakes of past failed fisheries. Sustainability in the fishing industry touches me when I consider my children's future—it provides a choice for my children to continue a tradition that has been in our family for five generations. It is my hope that this book will help you discover exactly where your seafood comes from, and the impact of your choices.

This project has turned into one of the biggest learning experiences of my life. I would like to attribute that largely to both Jen and Jeff, who have taught me more than any workshop or training program could ever offer. It is important that I thank Melinda Auger, Tuula Pohto, and Lil and Dave Siider; without their superior love and care for my children, I couldn't have carried this through. Thanks to Carmen, John and Vicky, Stephanie, Mom, and all of my trustworthy proofreading friends. Thanks to Sarah Martin, Kim West, and Tom Havloc for answering all my questions. To all the staff at Living Oceans Society; Aaron, Oonagh, Susan, Bruce, Randy, Dana, Elicia, Jen, and Jeff, who all contributed to this book in many ways. Thanks to all the people who contributed their recipes and provided information. This book wouldn't have been possible with out you.

Most of all, I'd like to thank those at home for putting up with the things that come from having a working mama, such as sandwiches for dinner, mismatched socks, rushed mornings to get everyone out the door, and the odd bit of crankiness!

—Karen Sommer

LIVING OCEANS SOCIETY is a non-profit organization based in Sointula, British Columbia, committed to the preservation of marine biological diversity and the creation of sustainable fisheries through the establishment of marine protected areas and ecosystem management of our oceans. Proceeds from the sale of this book will be devoted to the society's sustainable fisheries campaign.

For more information, please contact Living Oceans Society at:

Box 166
Sointula, B.C. Canada
V0N 3E0
Tel: (250) 973-6580
Fax: (250) 973-6581

Become a friend of Living Oceans Society

Your generous support will help Living Oceans Society develop and implement programs designed to protect our ocean.

Copy this form and return to: Living Oceans Society, Box 166, Sointula, BC Canada, V0N 3A0; fax (250) 973-6581.

Name: _____ Address: _____

City: _____ Province/State: _____ Postal Code: _____

Phone: _____ Fax: _____ Email: _____

Choose Your Species

❏	$10.00	Wolf Eel	❏	$200.00	Steller Sea Lion
❏	$30.00	Red Irish Lord	❏	$500.00	King Crab
❏	$50.00	Killer Whale	❏	$1000.00	Giant Octopus
❏	$100.00	Tiger Rockfish	❏	_____	Other